THE MEMOIR

THE RIVER OF LIFE

By

Dr. Sofia Laurden-Davis Adams

Copyright © 2023

All Rights Reserved

Dedication

First, I would like to give thanks to the Lord for giving me a challenging, wonderful life journey. This book is especially dedicated to my children, grandchildren, and great-grandchildren from the time this Memoir was written. This book is also dedicated to my husband, Cameron, who became my companion and editor of my manuscript. We travel together and enjoy our God-given talents in art, wood art, book writing, music, and investing in real estate. All the way through hardships and good times, we are bonded, help one another, and enjoy life while living here on this earth of plenty. I also want to give thanks to all the individuals whom I loved before and who were with me as part of my life, one person at a time.

My parents, who gave me a chance to become independent at the beginning of my life, are a big part of these experiences of mine. I truly treasure every experience I went through because without those experiences I went through, I would not be the person I am today. The key to a successful life is to learn from experiences and reframe events from negative experiences to turn them into positive ones to live a good life. Thank you all.

Finally, now in my life, Cameron has been my husband since November 2022; I am thankful for meeting Cameron, and being married to him is absolutely a wonderful life experience. I have enjoyed traveling and camping to witness the Lord's creation here on earth, which I call it; I am now experiencing the *"Light At The End of the Tunnel."* I love you, my dear husband, Cameron Adams. I am thankful to the Lord that I met you at the end of the bridge; there is light. Amen.

Acknowledgment

I would like to express gratitude to my dear husband, Cameron, for being with me while editing this book, "The Memoir: The River of Life. who was rereading my manuscript and asking questions that helped me to see it and correct it. I am thankful for the ups and downs in my life that put my life geared towards prosperity. I learned how to survive many struggles and knowledge the Lord had given me, and I was able to develop my strengths, and I learn skills in life to survive. Without it, I would never be who I am today. Challenges in life make you stronger, and we learn skills while heading to prosperity. THANK YOU.

Contents

Prologue

This book is a compilation of my life experiences from when I was a young child and up to this point of age in the 60s. Life can be challenging, and those challenges I have encountered become my tools to be stronger than ever. I became immune to hardships and difficulties, but instead, it made me more knowledgeable of unknown circumstances. Life challenges I have experienced should be treasured for a lifetime. I based those life experiences on improving my situation and life circumstances to a higher level. I went through many storms in life, treacherous life, and its environment and community, and it continues the journey I must wiggle the best to live a comfortable life till these days I became skillful at passing through difficulties with ease.

INTRODUCTION

First, understanding my life journey is through much thankfulness to God for my given strength, faith, endurance, challenges, struggles, and the opportunity to move forward with the Lord's guidance no matter how the circumstances are. I believe that I am meant to live to these days due to faith, strength, and endurance given by our Almighty. From when I was young until these days of my life, I have finally achieved my longing to be educated at a higher level. In the beginning, I felt so strange when someone called me Dr. Davis, my previous husband's last name, and now Dr. Adams, or Dr. Sofia, and I would say, really? You deserve it, Sofia, to be called Doctor," One of my colleagues said.

I was awarded and graduated with my doctoral the year in 2014. I finished and published my dissertation, which transformed into a manuscript titled "Nepotistic Ideology in Nonprofit and For-profit Family-owned and operated organization" through ProQuest at Capella University in the School of Public Service and Leadership. My degree in the highest education ever as a PhDs I specialized in the Management of Nonprofit Agencies and Leadership in Human Services. My dissertation was transformed into a manuscript and was one of few chosen by Scholars' Press, the Academic Publisher, to be published through them and translated into seven different world languages. I have written and published seven books so far, which you can find on my website, www.drsofiaadams.com. Then, the adventure in book writing continues until these days of my age in the 60s. Also, I am continuing my volunteering at the Guardian Ad Litem Program to protect neglected and abused children in America.

Before I got to this point of my journey here on earth of plenty, I was a single parent and went through hunger with my two children in the USA, the land of plenty. I was not approved for food stamps and help from the government because I owned lands in Ocala, Florida, and I used to work in big companies, When divorce happened with my now ex-husband in year 1997, I quit my job due to too many work hours. I stay home with my two children instead. Then we went to hunger. I met Thomas in 1998. While I was struggling to keep up with my house mortgage, Thomas invited me to stay with him in his 3 bedroom home with my children. I agreed. But I need to know him first before I will be able to engage with him in that manner. After getting to know each other, we got married. We opened businesses together, reopened the trucking business, the limousine, and the mortgage closing. Then the journey begins.

Since we moved from New Jersey to Bonifay, Florida, Thomas and I have built businesses again here in Florida. He brought his trucking business knowledge from New Jersey to Panhandle, Florida. He continued his trucking business, and I built my own business called Human Enterprise. I became the founder of Bonifay Guild for the Arts, Inc., in the year 2004, Laurden Davis and Associates, Sofia's Fine Art Studio, Laurden-Davis Art Gallery, Mortgage Closer/Signing, Rental Properties, and Notary Public Service. That's before COVID-19. Covid-19 created a big impact on our lives. But recently, writing this memoir, I tried to come back again to rebuild my business, but everything is not the same. I have now become a real estate investor, a fine artist, and a writer. Thomas passed away in December 2020 from falling at rehab. Parkinson's and dementia added to too much suffering from diseases in life, and he can't go on.

Remembering the past of my life was sad and amazing, too. I also graduated from Northcentral University for Best Practices Teaching Online; I am ahead of the game. I thought I would be knowledgeable in teaching the best practices in an online setting. Although a hybrid style of teaching was less in demand at the time I was taking the certification to teach online, I am excited to tap into a different world of teaching. When I was young, education was and is still very important to me. To continue my journey, I must have faith, strength, and endurance.

Therefore, by knowing the other side of myself by rebuilding my compassion for other people, faith, and getting back to focus on others' needs, again, I will survive through my journey in life with purpose. At the beginning of my life as a ten-year-old child, I was always innocently looking for the Lord to guide me as my parents taught me how to always pray. Today, I have visualized previous experiences as my tools to survive and live a prosperous life.

In July 2022, I met a man whom I love, and I enjoy traveling all over the USA and enjoying the beauty we are surrounded by God's creation here on earth of plenty. His name is Cameron. Cameron is also a retired individual and active in creating wood art carving. We got married in November 2022. You can also find him on his website, www.cameron-adams.com. We are planning to travel internationally and continue our creative minds to design more art pieces together.

CHAPTER ONE

Born into River of Life

Once we are born into the world of life, we go through many ups and downs, which are like water flowing through rocks, mud, and falling branches, and maybe, shall we say, like a river of life. However, some will reject the flow of the water, and some will just go with the flow. I am thankful to the Lord for guiding me with my life pursuit and listening to the flow of the water that carries me to where I am supposed to be.

I can remember how I came out of this world; I am amazed that I am still standing at my age in my 60s, when I was born on July 11, 1957, struggles of coming out to see the world had already existed. Such experiences I came out from my mother's womb to live in this world of plenty. From the moment I was born, the struggle I had encountered and the struggle to survive was a measure of choice whether I would live, die, or be reborn from the past.

One day, my mother was ready to give birth to me as the third child among six sisters. It was 4:30 in the morning, and I was about to come out into the world from my mother's womb. My parents' previous generation, and traditionally, there was no Medical Doctor or emergency vehicle to carry my mother to the hospital, but the birth process was through a midwife. A midwife has no education in birthing a baby, but a midwife has just the skills and compassion to help. My father called a midwife, calling not through the phone but to walk 15 kilometers at night or in the middle of the night through woody forests, bushes, and wild animals.

In those years, there was no specialized doctor as a gynecologist, and people in that era had to call a midwife to give birth to a baby. There were no lights on the street. My father must go through the process of walking in the dark to get a midwife. My parents lived in a place where it was half uncivilized community in the years of the 1920s. My birth year was 1957. In those eras, just like my father's experiences, he would walk 15 to 25 kilometers to get to the midwife's house. There were no telephones or cell phones then. The side of the streets with tall grass and trees were overwhelmingly grown. The only light my father had been using was the bottle of Coke containing kerosene and braided cloth. My father would run and walk at the same time to get there faster to the midwife's house in the rain and wind blowing the only light he had. Finally, he got there from 4 am to 5:30 in the morning. It took an hour plus another hour to get to where my mother gave birth to me.

On the other hand, my mother was struggling to labor the third child in the family, me. In a hurry, my father forgot to close the door tightly when he got out of the house to get the midwife. While my mother was screaming in pain, the door would hit on the other end. The wind was playing against the door while my two sisters were watching our mother's cry of pain to give birth to me. Our mother took a long piece of string made of "boli," a kind of palm tree, to make mats. She tied the "boli" up on the ceiling to help her in pain, birthing me. I think I was in pain in the behind when my mother was giving birth to me. I had that pain when Mom gave birth to me; I can still feel it these days. I treasured the memorable moment to remember my life today and her journey of birthing me.

Since I was young at 11 years of age, I was already a financial help for my family. I did babysit and gave my income to my parents, who these days still give money to put my nieces and nephews to school. With a PhDs in the United States of America and my accomplishments in considered a stable situation, I am still the financial help for my family, now including my nieces and nephews put to school to be educated to survive out there in jobs.

To continue birthing me, finally, the midwife came in and saw my mother birthing, holding the string attached to the post. My mother answered and screamed, telling the midwife that the baby, me, was coming out. The midwife told my mother to relax and lie down so the midwife could help to take me out of the womb. The midwife was instructing my father to give more light to what she was holding. The midwife must see me if my head is already out from the womb. But my head did not go out first, but my two legs. The midwife said to have my mother be brought to the hospital because I would not be able to make it due to two legs coming out first. The town I was born in was very secluded to everything, such as the nearest town, neighbors, hospital, and away from civilization.

There were no vehicle lights on the streets and only three visible neighbors in the area. The streets were all made of big stones, too rugged terrain, and impossible to rush walking on the road and bushy terrain. There was no electricity, no telephones, and no washing machines. At that time, the family washed clothes in the river. All we had were each other, and food sources were through farming. My mother cried and was in pain and wanted the midwife to remove the baby, me, from her. Two legs first to come out from the womb is very difficult. The midwife was having difficulty trying to take me out without damage. Despite struggles and difficulties, I finally came out into this world.

However, the journey continues. The memoir explains the life I went through like a river where water is flowing. The water flows continuously without stopping. It keeps going whether the water movements hit piles of stones, tree branches, or many other elements the water may encounter. Until these days, the flow of the water continues, but just lately, it has changed course. With the

Lord's guidance, I ended up in a smooth, very different type of lifestyle with freedom and with my own plans and goals with dance, which I adore. I have believed in the Lord's guidance since I was young; I am and still am an overcomer and a winner.

At the beginning of life, my parents were my guidance in life. My father was a photographer, and my mother was a beautician and a businessperson. I learned how to sell fish from my mother's entrepreneurial mind. When I was 10 years of age, I would go with my mother to buy fish at the boat dock. I would sell these fish in our neighborhood. I had a basket full of fish I would carry from house to house. I learned how to earn income at the age of 10 years old. Every time my mother and I rode on the jeepney at 4 a.m., I saw my mother praying while we were inside the jeepney. While growing up, I imitated my mother in praying everywhere I went.

Also, I can remember when I was ten years old, and I had a fever of 110. I was taken care of by my mother's organic medicine, such as grass growing in our backyard and heating it up until the grass was heated up and placed on my forehead. I was somehow cured. That early morning at 3 a.m., I was dreaming. My dream was about a silver color airplane with red doors flying in the sky. I was trying to catch that airplane, and I still remember those days when I was bigger than this airplane that I was dreaming about. I was a giant child, and the airplane was much smaller than me. I told my father about my dream, and my father told me, which I will never forget,

"You are going to places such as America." I asked what is and where America is, and my father said, "America is heaven." I continued telling my father about my dream.

In the year 1969, I was only 12 years old when my father, Eutiquio, started to get sick. He was paralyzed, his right hand unable to move. He fell from the coconut tree while climbing to harvest from our coconut farm. However, he was trying to stand up to move and kept moving, and I learned from him that he was unable to carry himself fully due to the fact that he would drag himself while walking. I always helped my father walk, but while walking every morning, he managed to walk by himself. When my father went to our farm, I would follow him and watch him.

In the year 1991, my father, Eutiquio, passed away without me because I was in the USA at the time when he passed away. I came to the USA in the year 1984, assigned to World Expo 84 in New Orleans. I was in Hawaii in the year 1991 and went back home to attend his burial. Stayed there for 2 weeks and went back to Hawaii. They waited for me to come home before burying my dear father. When I saw my papa in a coffin, I almost fainted, and my cousin Primo rescued me from falling to the ground. My Papa will not be forgotten.

Crying while writing this Memoir, remembering my father as my strength and guidance while growing up and is still to these days. I am always my father's baby girl. I missed you, Papa, so much that it breaks my heart every time I remember when I was young, at the time when I was nearby, always watching him while talking with animals in the wild. I would see him talking to birds and deer when he sees passing through the yard and backyards. I do the same these days in my now 60s years of age. Imagine carrying my Papa's mentality and the activity I witnessed growing up; such an amazing, memorable moment that is difficult to forget.

Family unity is an important bridge to bring back good memories to share and, of course, to treasure for life. We only have one parent, and we must treasure the memories we encountered with our family and the time when we leave this earth of plenty; precious memories never fail. My father used to read the Bible with people coming to our store every morning. He would prepare himself to sit on the bench, and here came the people just to talk, but he ended up reading Bibles with my father. I am also the same today, but with a new way of sharing the Word of God, through Prayer Is Powerful group from 20 members to now more than 300 members at the time when this book was written, continually growing more and more. I would send my devotional reading and prayer through Facebook Messages and Messenger pages. I am still seeking more people to participate in my group, Prayer Is Powerful group.

When my Papa got sick after he fell from climbing a coconut tree, it seemed everything was on my mother's shoulder in taking care of all of us and the farm my father left behind due to sickness. The shadows of memories and their future seem to follow my mother to tackle life while my father goes through being paralyzed before he passes away. My Papa's photography darkroom has been neglected and empty. I could remember when my father was still alive and one day when my sisters and I dressed up pretending to be class socialites smoking cigarettes. I was only 11 years old, and my sisters were 12 and 14. My Papa was curious about what we were doing in his dark photography room. He knocked on the door many times, but we didn't open the door. Therefore, my father went to the other room to get the key to the darkroom and opened the door with his key. He opened the door and saw us and what we were doing. He saw us with cigarettes in our mouths, wearing socialite clothes with high-heeled shoes.

My father pulled the cigarette from our mouths; although not lit, he slapped our mouths lightly, and this was never forgotten that until these days, I have never ever touched a cigarette, including my sisters. All of us do not smoke and do not drink alcohol. The lesson learned was amazing because I shared these lessons with my children today. My children do not smoke and do not drink alcohol. These experiences I had when I was young carried over now that I am 65 years of age.

My dear father was paralyzed due to injury from falling from a coconut tree. I then learned how to become a financial help for my parents. I was only 12 years of age in the year 1969. I was already helping my family to earn income. Then, when my father passed away in 1991, I was continually chosen to help my mother earn income to support the whole family. When I was very young, my father passed away, and he still is to this day; I became an entrepreneur, being self-employed.

CHAPTER TWO

My Father Said, "America Is Heaven"

When I was 10 years old as a child, I could remember my father telling me a story about America. That night, I had a high fever. I slept well after my parents took care of me by giving me organic medicine, such as the grass in our backyard, and my mother would put it on top of a fire and then place this grass on my forehead. That night, I was relieved, and I slept well. In the middle of the early morning, around 3 a.m., I woke up due to my dreams, such as a fairytale. My dream was about a silver-red airplane flying in the sky, and I was a giant child trying to catch the airplane. I can see myself as a giant child trying to catch the airplane up in the sky. I woke up my father and told him about my dream.

My father immediately interpreted my dream. He said, "You are going places in other countries." At age 10, I was already thinking, where am I going when I grow up? My father said, "Your dream means you are going to America!? I asked my father, "What is America, Papa?" At 10 years of age, I have no idea what and where America is. Innocently, I responded to my father with puzzling questions as if America was my godmother. My father immediately answered me, "America is Heaven, and you are going there in the near future." My eyes were lit up, and I wondered where I was going in America and what is America. As I picture in my mind what my father says, America is heaven; therefore, I picture and see images in my mind that I will see angels in America. It was amazing to hear from my father when I was young that America is a rich country. He also added that there are no poor and hungry people in America. There is no crime in America, as my father explained that America is heaven. People living in America are kind people, and they are rich.

Until these days, I am still puzzled about America. All I knew about America when I was young was America is heaven, according to my dear father. When I came to America in the year 1984 at age 27 years old, my mind seemed to have gone back to my childhood of what my Papa had said. When I landed at the American airport, I saw tall white people with blue and green eyes and long noses, and I immediately hugged all I encountered the tall and white people in the airport. I greeted them with a smile, arms wide open, and such an exciting voice. Saying the greeting with the word *"Hi"* was not just a two-letter word, but *"Hiiiiiiiii…"* with a big smile, enthusiastic, and excited childlike voice ready to hug the angels I have encountered in the airport. I also encountered a black woman, and I was reluctant to hug her because my father didn't tell me that there is other colored skin like mine in America. However, she was so nice and hugged me anyway. She said, "God bless you, honey," and I was so puzzled by what I had learned from my father. Because my father said only white people I would see here in America, and they are angels. My friends were so surprised by my behavior, hugging all the people at the airport, especially the white people I met at the airport in year 1984.

To my curiosity about cultures in America, in 1992, back in New Jersey from Hawaii, I studied Liberal Arts and Photography in 1996, and I focused on Social Behavior, Arts, Cultures, American History, and legendary people who came to America at the beginning of Americans living here in the land of plenty. I found out that America, or shall we call America the "United States of America" (USA), has mixed cultures coming from many different countries in the world. To continue my experiences as a naïve foreign-born girl living on American soil now for more than 39 years, I am still puzzled by what my father said because I am a Guardian Ad Litem volunteer, and I have encountered so many white people who are struggling, and children with blond hair in hunger and abandoned.

Whether your skin color is white, brown, yellow, or black, it does not matter. What matters is who we are within us as an individual person, not by skin color. Also, for us to move forward in our life pursuits and lifestyle, we must choose what's right in our journey in life. We are just temporary here on earth of plenty, but there are so many choices living in this world. We must make sure that we choose the right direction with God's guidance and be thankful for all the blessings we receive every day.

THE MEMOIR: THE RIVER OF LIFE

I am so thankful that I met those angels when I came to America in the year 1984 as one of the Chinese hired workers at World Expo 84 in New Orleans. I am here on American soil, and surely, I am blessed. I prayed every day and always be thankful for what I have on this earth of plenty. I was able to continue my education here in America, which, since I was young, was my goal to pursue at a higher level. I am now a doctor, as we call it, a Philosophy Doctor (PhDs) in Human Services, Management, and Leadership. I then continue my pursuit to move forward. You may ask how that happened in America in Heaven, as my father said.

When I was young, at 10 years of age, I had a fever of 110, and I was dreaming about an airplane with silver and red color airplane up in the sky. I got married to Cameron in November 2022; I then made my wedding dress and decoration of my wedding in color silver and red. To continue, I tried to catch this airplane in my dream, and I saw my child's body, but I was bigger than the airplane up in the sky. It was an amazing dream. Until these days, I unconsciously repeated the colors of red and gray as I would buy gray color dresses. My wedding dress is gray in color, and the cabana door and walls are based on red and gray, the color of the airplane I dreamed of when I was 10 years of age.

My mind was ingrained with the name "America is Heaven," and until these days, I tell stories to everyone. I still remember those memories and what my father had told me. We may have to analyze what is "heaven." The interpretation of the word "heaven" in my own version of what heaven is all about is that heaven is the place of success and how we live here on earth of plenty. I could remember when I was young, I was already ingrained in being an entrepreneur.

As a child, I used to go with my mother to buy fish in the ocean on the boat ramp, waiting for fishermen who were the wholesalers selling fish. Once we had the fish, we would come home and sell these fish to our neighborhood. My mother would prepare a towel; she would twist it around to fit on my head to carry the big basket full of bubbling fresh anchovies. The basket was full of bubbling anchovies still alive, and the water from the basket would drop onto my hair and shoulder down to my clothes. When I came back from selling fish, my mother would say to change my wet clothes, so I don't get sick. She would then count the money, and she would give me my salary, and that would be the money I saved. Since then, when I was young, I developed this type of personality and activity on how to earn income.

This entrepreneurial mind brought me to these days of being self-employed.

Of course, I decided to be self-employed due to too much time working, and I had no time for my children, ages 5 and 8, at that time. I used to work at first; in 1984, I was hired by a Chinese

Company to represent their handmade carpet and rehired and worked with the same company in New York. Then moved on to Germany, worked with the Army Community Service, then to Hawaii from 1989 to 1992, worked at First Hawaiian Bank, then to New Jersey from 1992 to 2004, and worked with K. Hovnanian, the big real estate developer in the USA, and Federal Credit Union in New Jersey.

The cost of living is expensive in New Jersey, so I worked two jobs, full-time and part-time, with Federal Credit Union. These experiences made it a stepping stone to becoming self-employed and becoming an entrepreneur. Moving from New Jersey to the Florida Panhandle, I continued my self-employed status and opened a nonprofit organization called Bonifay Guild for the Arts, Inc., a 501C3, while continuing my PhDs. in Human Services, specializing in Management and Leadership. My dissertation was transformed into a manuscript and published and was selected by Scholar's Press, Academic Publisher, to be published. I was fortunate. That's what I call "heaven" here on earth.

Although I am 66 years of age, I still act in childlike behavior. Laughter and enjoying life wherever I am and what the Lord has given to all humanity; you may be surprised that we have everything already in life. We must see and look through our own senses, good common sense, and good wisdom, and carry good consciences within us that the Lord has given to all humans here on earth of plenty, then we truly in heaven. That's my interpretation of heaven. In the other book that I published lately, titled "The Two Universes of Self," the Thought Universe is huge and vague, and the Physic Universe takes the visual action that all humanity can see. The unseen universe, the Thought Universe, contains so many choices that cannot be seen. It depends on your choices in life. the Physic (Phyzeek) Universe acts usually, and the result affects the Self Universe. So, what are your choices in life?

My choice in life was fulfilled as I completed my doctoral PhDs , and I educated myself to a higher level, which, since my younger years, was my main goal in life. Although I went through many disasters in life and different roads, which were not my goals, I went through it, passed it, and moved on. Whatever happened in my life along the journey, I am still focused on what my goals are. I did and I made it. Since I was young, I was already an entrepreneur with my mother's guidance. I then brought it up until these days that I became self-employed, as you've read in my book titled "Entrepreneurial Minds: Root Causes to Branch Out Are Through Educations and Experiences." Check it out. Go to www.drsofiaadams.com

CHAPTER THREE

I Bit My Boss

Since I was appointed to help my mother in the financial area due to my father being unable to fully function in his business as a photographer, at the young age of 12 years old, I was babysitting this couple with two children. The husband and wife were music teachers. My mother has already taken 3 months of my salary in advance. I was forced to work until 3 months paid off. Working with this couple, taking care of their 2 young children, ages 4 and 6 years old, was a challenge after finding the house of danger I was in.

One day, I was in the living room picking up some stuff the children scattered all over the floor after playing games with them, and then I prepared them to take a nap. I heard my boss, the father of the children I babysit, calling me. He said to pick up something here in the other bedroom where he was. I then went to the bedroom where he was. Suddenly, I was pulled inside, and the room was locked inside. To my surprise, he was naked. I was very frightened and was forced, and my boss grabbed my two hands to touch him all over. I was afraid and fought back by pushing him away, but he was stronger than me at 12 years of age; I started to cry. As a 12-year-old girl, I had no idea how the man's body and his own private scared me so much, but at the same, I was curious about his nature.

Today, as in the 60s, such memories brought me this time of awareness and avoidance due to my experiences and curiosity. I still encounter men who want to put me in bed. I avoided them all, and my thought processes through my experiences when I was young and my parents' teaching about "no sex before marriage" flashes in my mind, giving me a warning to watch out and be careful and put in the self-respect within myself. It was and is always my parents' guidance and lectures about avoiding sexual activity and having self-respect that put me on the safer side of life while growing up as a lady. Sexual activity is only when a woman is married to a man whom she marries.

It seems that I am going back to my childhood experiences, and it brought me back to then when, now in my 60s and a widow living by myself, encountered these types of events still exist. Not that I am afraid of men, I do like men, but I need respect, and pursuing, and forcing me to do what they want me to do for them, or he will NOT work for me. I respect myself, and I want them to respect me as well. For me, sexual intimacy is a sacred activity for a man and a woman as a married couple, as my parents told me when I was growing up. Therefore, I must marry a man before having sexual intimacy.

Then, before marrying, I must select a responsible man with self-respect, according to my parents, and therefore, marriage will last, and it should last forever. I will never forget the very important information about passion versus purity. I have learned that from a very young age. When I was 12 years old, my first experience with my boss gave me more lessons to learn about men; these days, my life is a long journey, and it continues even to my older days, that *no sex until marriage is performed.*

The scariest of all was when I was a frightened little girl who almost fainted on the floor at the time when my boss started touching me all over. I crawled towards the door and grabbed the knob lock, and opened it. He came after me and held the door and hugged me behind; with his nature, I can feel that hardness of his private being, so to speak. I then bit his hands and arms, and he got hurt; that released me from his strong arms and hands, and I was able to get out. He was angry, I could hear his voice, and I was so afraid.

Finally, after many struggles to get out and unlock the door, I opened the door and ran towards the kitchen and through the backyard, and I was crying all night long. I ran and ran farther away from him. I ended up in the garden where I could hide from him. Being afraid and watching all my footsteps while running, I stumbled onto a stone in the garden. I was hurt and wounded, but it really didn't matter; what mattered to me at that moment was to run away. The wounded, bleeding foot of mine didn't matter; I kept running until I disappeared from the eyes of a predator, my boss.

Time passed by; they were looking for me and found me in the garden and asked me why I was in the garden this late at night. What is going on? There were no answers coming from my mouth because I did not know what to say. I remember my boss was telling me not to say anything at all about what had happened or I would be fired. I was very frightened that I would be fired because my parents had taken three months' salary.

Although there was nothing major happening, only touches, I could not look at his face due to fear and shame. Fear of this man repeating his plan and shame of my curiosity as a little girl at 12 years old. It seemed my life was in a danger zone, and I could not breathe, especially when my boss would stare at me, and it seemed danger was back again. I would run again and stay away from my boss. He would call my name, but I pretended I did not hear him. After the 3 months' salary advance was paid off, I was so happy to get out of that place where I was so very scared and ashamed of being there. I went home, and no one knew about my experience being there at the *house of danger*. I hope that after my boss was bitten by me, he no longer messes around with young girls.

Until these days after my beloved previous husband, whom I had married for 22 years, who passed away on December 17, 2020, I was alone and living by myself. Being a widow, there are always men who want to date me. I tried to avoid them all. So, I'd rather be living alone, so to speak. Learning from the experiences

I had when I was 12 years of age and so on, now in my 60s, I have that hesitation to engage quickly with another man in my life. But of course, there are temptations that come with all those avoidances. The memories of when I was growing up, such as being almost in the hands of someone who would take advantage of a vulnerable girl or a woman, are never forgotten until these days.

I was looking for a man with self-respect and who treated me as a special woman in his life, not just someone to play with like a toy. I am not that type of a woman, and I have never been well since I was young. I respect myself, and *self-worth* is very important. I always remember my parents' teaching about "no sex before marriage." Even in my old age, when I got married to my previous husband, Thomas Davis, in my 50s, before going to bed, it took 6 months to years before engaging in bed. That's me. After being alone in my cabana for many months, I met a respectful man who became my husband and got married in November 2022; his name is Cameron.

When I was young, no one really knew about my experiences when I was growing up until these days now that I am a writer and the opportunity to write it all will be a big surprise how I suffered and survived while I was growing up to these days of my life. But then I realized it was truly a huge benefit, for I became stronger and more powerful to face hardship in life. However, I do believe that the Lord was always with me because I always survived whatever hardship I went through. Writing all of it down also gives me the opportunity to heal the painful and fearful past that I always appreciate, and I am very thankful for everything I have these days. The River of Life: The Memoir book is truly a recognition of what I have accomplished in life despite the struggles that came along with it. After my boss was bitten by me, I hoped that he would never act like this type of activity to young girls anymore.

CHAPTER FOUR

Survival Skills At Kawasan Waterfall: Silence Prevail

At age 13, my uncle Felipe, whom we called Papa Felipe, adopted me when I came back from the family I worked with. Papa Felipe, the brother of my father, had a bus business called "Alagon." His wife was an elementary teacher, Mama Costan. Mama Costan and my uncle Felipe have one child, a boy named Ellie. Ellie drives a motorcycle and would bring me to school, and I would ride on his motorcycle. These days, in my 60s, I still love to ride a motorcycle, and sometimes, now, as a widow, I am tempted to be a friend of a man who has a motorcycle or is able to drive a motorcycle. When I met Thomas in the year 1997, he was always riding in his Harley Davidson Sporter. And I then joined him riding his sporter Harley Davidson motorcycle, and I enjoyed every moment with him. However, in December 2020, I became a widow, and I missed those activities we had together. I then decided to buy a motorcycle, and I already had someone to drive it for me. However, I will explain that later in the next chapter on what had happened.

My survival at Kawasan the Waterfall experience: I used to live with my uncle Felipe when I was 13 years of age. I am my aunt's girlchild. Wherever she goes, I am always with her. One day, my sister, Annie, came back from Manila to visit the family. Annie invited all her friends to have a picnic in *"Kawasan."* Kawasan is a beautiful waterfall scenery. The small Island where I was born is called Bohol Island. Bohol Island contains wonderful views like Hawaii, the Bahamas, and other islands with those types of sceneries.

When I was a young child, no one knew or discovered this place where Chocolate Hills was a popular tourist destination. Today, the place has already been discovered by vacationers, resort companies, beach enthusiasts, and tourism researchers. Nearby, there is a sight called "Sea Of Clouds." This insight has given me the interest to invest in the area where I was born and left this area for more than 39 years. Now in my 60s, I am tempted to go back and plan to open businesses such as tourism business.

In the corner of this Island, there was a green mountain full of beautiful views. Green tall trees, green grass, waterfalls, and crystal clear water trees cover part of the beautiful river. On the left and the right side of the river were trees with large heart-shaped leaves. At the front side of the river, there were big black rocks, gray stones, and white sand on the ground. Above the river, opposite the front side, there was Rocky River Mountain, where the waterfall comes from, down to the middle of the river. This Rocky River Mountain was very high, probably 2,000 feet.

If one stayed under the waterfall and this person was not strong enough to hold, this person would drown due to the volume of the waterfall, which is heavier than tons of steel. As far as I know, nobody wants to stand under the waterfall due to the strong flow of the water. People stay only on the other side of the river. I insisted and went with my sister Anne and her friends no matter what would happen.

I was very interested to be with my sister and her friends to enjoy the view of the Kawasan Waterfall. Therefore, Annie has the responsibility to notify our Uncle Felipe that I will be going with them. However, Annie, my dear sister, insisted I stay home because the waterfall is a very dangerous place to be in. I insisted and explained to my sister Annie that I knew how to swim. My sister Annie would say that she would not be responsible for my recklessness. While my dear sister Annie was talking to me, I was ignoring all her concerns and disagreement about my coming with them to Kawasan Waterfall Island. Instead, I ran back to Uncle Felipe's house to notify him of my plan to be with my sister Annie and friends at Kawasan Waterfall. It didn't take long. I came back quickly and helped my sister Annie with excitement to prepare for the travel to Kawasan Waterfall.

I then went to our mom's store and picked up a few packs of biscuits and 2 packs of soda drinks. For snacks, I meant to select crackers with a cellophane cover. I put these selected snacks in the bag. Enthusiastic about moving on to start heading with my friends to Kawasan Waterfall, I intently hid the cracker under the sodas and clothes so no one could take it. Everybody was ready to go to Kawasan, a waterfall in Bohol Island, where I was born. I was very excited to swim in a river with crystal clear water until my sister Annie told me to always stay with her. Despite my sister's warnings and precautions, I was moving faster to get to our destination. We've walked past the rice fields, vegetable gardens, rice terraces, forest, green trees, and birds singing up in the trees and flying above us.

It took more than an hour for us to get to our destination. I would rest and sit on the grass, and sometimes, I would run after them to catch up. I was having a great time seeing the view and hearing birds singing, but my legs were hurting due to a long walk. But overcoming pain and being so excited, I would scream loudly after seeing from a distance the beautiful waterfall. I could hear the noise of the water falling from the rock and was pleased by the crystal-clear water flowing down into the middle of the river.

My journey to Kawasan with my sister Annie and her friends when I was 13 years of age, and despite the distance from where we were, it was clear to me to see the beautiful river and water flowing on the rocks. When our friends and my sister got almost near the waterfall, I climbed up on top of a stone near the river and stood up facing the waterfall. I shouted very loudly and said the word "helllloooo!" waving my two little hands facing the waterfall. Anyway, nobody heard my loud, enthusiastic voice.

I was almost at the side of the waterfall where the deeper water area was when my sister Annie saw me and lifted her left arm up and down, anchoring her hips, her right finger, pointing right at me. My sister Annie was coming towards me with her opened wide eyes, staring at me. It seemed my sister Annie was angry about something. The expression of her body language and looking at her lips while talking was the only way to communicate with each other. Annie was so angry because I was close to the deep water. The only way my sister can communicate with me is to come near to me and our body language from a distance.

Annie didn't want me to come with them in the first place. I was a child who would keep moving and had no hesitation to step in for exploration. I am now grown up, in my 60s, and still moving forward. My sister Annie would grab my hands and settle me down for a while, and she would try to put me in shallow water under the tree. Probably, my sister wants to tie me up in the tree to settle down or to slow down. The word *slowdown* is a very special word that will be explained in another chapter of this book.

When I was 12 years of age, my sister Annie would watch me and settle me down in shallow water on the other side of the river, which was the opposite side of where she was. Our friends went to the area where the exciting side of the river, such as the surge of the waterfall, was stronger. However, I felt like it was not fair to stay in the shallow water. So, I decided to go to the middle of the river when I had the opportunity to stay away from my sister's sight.

Today, as in my 60s, I am somehow challenged when it comes to struggles. Challenges in life make me more capable, and I feel like my capability is tested and my strength in resolving issues is always renewed. When I was young, for example, I imagined the deep side of the waterfall would be exciting and waiting for me to come to that side to enjoy. I wasn't even thinking that I was going to the dangerous side of the river. I then looked around, and my little feet carried me towards the deep side of the river. I jumped and swam all the way to the middle of the river. After many lapses of swimming, I felt hungry, and I went to the baskets of food.

I looked around first to make sure no one saw me digging in the basket for food. I took out the hidden crackers inside the big bag of cellophane containers in the basket, hidden not to be seen. I quickly ate the crackers, removed all crackers from the cellophane bag, and placed those extra crackers in the basket. I brought the cellophane bag with me and rushed back to the water. I was excited to go back to swim with a cellophane bag in my mouth, using it as a balloon to float on the water. My purpose is to have fun swimming with a cellophane bag in my mouth.

It truly looked like fun having a cellophane bag in my mouth while swimming. Our friends noticed my activity was more exciting; therefore, they tried to grab the cellophane from me. Sol, one of my sister's friends, saw me swimming with the cellophane in my mouth. Sol went in my direction, swam rightfully to the water, and grabbed the cellophane from my mouth. However, I did not let go of the cellophane. This was where Sol would push me down hard under the water just to grab the cellophane I had. I did not let the cellophane be taken away from me. I would protect the cellophane by staying away from my sister's friend, Sol.

However, due to the pressure when I was under the water, which I needed the mouth to breathe, I then let the cellophane go, and I was able to breathe, which is the most important to stay alive. I have decided that the pressure was too much for keeping the cellophane. I started giving it away to save my life. I did not care about cellophane anymore, which was the most important at that moment in my life. I didn't care about the cellophane that would be taken away from me. For me, it was not fun anymore, and it was a life-and-death situation. I tried to breathe up from underneath the water to breathe, but Sol vigorously held my head and pushed me back again into the water.

I was going down deeper and was pushed down more by the forces of the waterfall. In my mind, I only begged for help, but strong hands pushed me back down underwater repeatedly. I would scream and beg again to leave me alone, but only in my mind because underwater, no one could hear my plea. A thirteen year old girl started to pray, pray to the Lord to grant my life underwater, which still until these days I pray when I am in danger and confused in life, and started a group of Prayer Is Powerful 20, now more than 300 members now while writing this book of mine. I do believe and still believe that prayer is powerful.

Suddenly, my prayer was heard, and a miracle happened. You can bring prayer within your Thought Universe with you even if you are underwater and unable to breathe. The mind, which I call the spiritual being we have still and always existed within, in my book just published in the year 2021, the "Two Universes of Self," which I also plan to have a part 2 and will be titled "The Thought Universe."

"Please, somebody help! I am drowning! Oh! God, I'm going to die! Please help me!" Anyway, no one can hear my plea, but my prayer somehow has been heard by the Almighty. Although I cried because I was underwater, it seemed I was losing my breath. I was in a fearful situation. I was very frightened of the uncertainty of what would happen to me down under. The water was bubbling while I was screaming underwater, but no one understood me. My sister's friends, who saw the activity on the water, thought we were just playing and enjoying playing with the cellophane game on the water.

Obviously, nobody noticed that I was drowning. Sol got the cellophane, and I went all the way to the bottom of the river. Suddenly, I was abandoned and still struggling to survive, but instead, I focused on enjoying and seeing the elements underwater. These days, challenges in life are easy; having fun and excitement somehow in facing and solving life struggles and problems, I then become very skillful.

Anyway, while I was struggling to survive underwater, I saw beautiful things such as the white sand, the rocks with green weeds, the different kinds of fish swimming, yellow leaves, water lilies, and many little and big shells. However, the most interesting of all were the tiny crabs swimming, and they were enjoying the feast in the water, playing with the beautiful different colors of shells and sand. The fishes were swimming and wiggling their tails; to me, it seemed they were very happy to see me swimming with them underwater. At that moment, my wish was if I could just talk to fish and crabs and explain to them my situation that I could not breathe underwater. I thought that if they could only help me to breathe and survive, such as to push me up to the surface, I would appreciate it.

However, to my dismay, they were only elements in the water, "they couldn't help me," I thought. "How could they be? How?" Suddenly, I focus on their little legs crawling and crawling and hiding in a big stone with weeds around it. The crawling small crabs stretched their legs against the weedy, slippery, and treacherous stones. Wait! It seemed like the crabs were telling me something. I then imitated the little crabs enjoying climbing up the stones, stretching their flat and fragile legs up in the weedy stone. These acts and images had given me the strength and ideas to survive underwater.

Struggling against the pressure of the waterfall from the rocky mountain above down to the bottom of the river, I found ideas on how to survive. However, my strength was not enough as the pounding current of the water pushed me down to the deeper side of the water. I was surprised at what I saw; the big hole in the middle of the river captivated my attention. The darkness of the hole scared me beyond belief as the terror of what my imagination visualized, and I feared that my breathing would end and I see the other side of the world. I thought, "I must not let myself be dragged into that hole," I promised myself not to be dragged into that dark hole.

The phrase "I must not let myself be dragged into that dark hole" was repeated, which motivated me to survive and to live until these days. As I tried my best to go near the rocks to put my little feet and tried to push, I was almost having a lifeless body, and trying to put my head up to get some air. I saw a rope wiggling, coming towards me. I tried to grab it but couldn't reach the rope.

While my hands were trying to fight the water gushing from the waterfall that pounded me all the way down to that dark hole underwater, I lost the rope twice. In an attempt for the fourth time, I saw the rope wiggle toward my direction. My strength was not enough to catch the rope; however, I managed to follow the rope where it was going. Seeing the crabs inserting their little legs, crawling, and climbing up the stones with holes, I then imitated the crabs. I pushed my two little feet against the water (imitating the little crabs' activity underwater) and followed the rope all the way to the edge of the river. Suddenly, I heard voices; it was my sister Annie's voice and her friends crying and screaming while helping me to come up to the surface.

"Please, come and hold my hand." My sister Annie said while she was crying.

I tried to reach her hand, but it slipped away, and I saw my sister Annie looking for stones that had holes in them. My sister Annie found the big stones with holes to put her fingers in to hold on. She put her four fingers in the holes with her left and right hand facing the stone and extended her right leg towards the water. I knew that my sister Annie didn't know how to swim, but she tried her best to save me from drowning. Finally, I was able to hold on to my sister's toes and pushed my lifeless little body towards my sister's right leg towards the right side for her to touch the stones.

I extended my two arms to reach the sharp, pointed stones, enough for me to hold on, and I lifted my head up to get some air to breathe. My sister Annie and her friends were able to grab me and carry me all the way to the sand, laid upside down to remove water from my lungs. They pushed my back to empty and removed water from my body. I saw my sister Annie and some of her friends crying as if they didn't know what to do. The people on the other end were gone in the middle of the incident. Some of the other people there were not part of the group. They thought we were just playing similarly the first time when we were grabbing the cellophane on the water.

I was rested, and water was removed from my body. And I stayed on the ground for a while and started thinking about what had happened. Suddenly, my sister Annie was angry and screamed at her friends for being negligent in the incident. Annie was so angry with Sol because of what she had done to me by grabbing the cellophane from my mouth while swimming, which created the accident. One of my sister's friends, Ernest, knew how to swim but didn't do anything. Ernest was nervous and panicked. Although the group and I were so quiet and just stared at one another, I felt relief. After I was rested and able to walk back home, the group and I started walking slowly with a feeling of defeat and sadness due to the incident.

Finally, before I stepped forward to go back home, I looked back at the beautiful waterfall. The view and the crystal-clear water, the rocks, the trees, and, of course---the memory that will never be forgotten of what I had encountered in this place called "Kawasan," the waterfall of Bohol Island.   I faced the waterfall once more and stayed for five minutes, asking myself— "how did I survive underwater?"

There were many questions in my mind that it took so long for me to put together what had happened underwater. I then continued walking and covered my head with shoal straight back home and never looked back. I sometimes peep through the shoal, the place where I was almost drowned, and then I would walk again but, in my mind, thinking that someday I would visit this beautiful place again.

"Come on, let's go!" My sister Annie commanded everyone. "What happened to you underwater? How come you took so long to come up? My sister Annie asked. "I can't believe you are still alive! Ernest said. "Did you breathe underwater? What did you do?" Felix asked. I looked at them--stared at them with no words to explain. I didn't answer their questions. However, my mind was busy thinking and believing that as humans-- a survival power already built in within everyone if we only believe. This beautiful "Kawasan," the waterfall in Bohol Island that was more than 60 years ago, is still vivid in my mind; a view of the beauty in the surrounding areas will never be forgotten. The insight I have found has developed the thought of personal power as a human. I had used it one day in that waterfall, believing that I could survive, and I did that day just in case this tragedy happened again. I know I will be able to survive. In relation to any type of struggle, we as humans will always be able to survive if we just believe. I did.

Tragedy has many life forms, and tapping and learning that our experiences in life are only to sharpen our skills in survival if our mind is able to believe in our capability. Struggles have given us all the lessons to learn to survive whatever the life journey takes us in this world. Believing in ourselves with God's guidance makes us more capable of surviving all struggles we may go through in this life journey in our temporary world, the earth. We all go through the process, not knowing what the outcome of our decision will be. We make mistakes, and we learn from them. We move forward, and through the process of moving forward, we learn. We become equipped with courage and strength. Strengths and courage that when life experience again struck at 13 years of age, I survived the "Fifteen Kilometers of Tears" is the next to be told which life experiences make us brave and bold.

CHAPTER FIVE

Fifteen Kilometers of Tears: Faith Has Been Developed

My life has been tested many times, and there are times I would like to quit, but there are spiritual enforces to keep me going. Feel that spiritual enforcement in my situation is giving me a clue there, and it is always sending a message in all my circumstances. I just need to pay attention to it. However, there are times I cannot pay attention due to so many things and elements that occupy my thoughts. Therefore, I stay still and think *nothing.* I start emptying my mind. Then, I will be able to see the *unseen* that has been occupying my senses and spirituality within my own self. Somehow, I could see and listen clearly to my guts and thoughts. But suddenly, I saw a Word that distracted my confusion and occupied my attention to what needed to be done to see that there were hopes of everything that had happened. Not only Words but also things we see that connect to what we are suffering about. Then, realization is about to enter our mind, or shall I say, *"thoughts."*

The 15 kilometers of tears from our house to where I worked pursuing my education, which was always our family goal to fulfill, was a painful memory but will never be forgotten. We always have goals to have a higher level of knowledge through education. Shall

I be a nurse? Shall I be a medical doctor or an attorney? In our family, for survival, education was always the plan and goal while growing up. However, when the flood threw away all our resources in farming, my parents started to sort out things on how to survive. My goal was still to continue my education, which, at that time, High School was not free. Therefore, I started looking for a job for me to continue my high school education. Finally, I found a family of seven with five children to babysit and do some housework at an age somewhere between 12-13.

From my parent's house to the place where I had to babysit for this family of 7, it is 15 kilometers away. Therefore, to continue my education, I had to walk 15 kilometers from my parents' house to Mr. and Mrs. Langamen to take care of their five children. The couple introduced me to their 4 young children to watch. I stared at their children to figure out my life with these four children to watch just to get my education. They were not friendly at all. "I don't want her to sit down with me." says the oldest daughter. "Not with me either." the second daughter said. "No way, no way, not with me." the youngest boy said. The mother said, "No. Listen. This is Sofia, and she will be your babysitter. You hear? Mrs. Langamen insisted. Aww, move. "No. There is no room." "Get away." The young girl was pinching me, and I said, "Stop pinching me," in a loving way of saying. After I was introduced to their children, I was thinking about whether I must continue my education or get away from these so mean young children.

After fifteen kilometers of travel, the tears never stopped. I cried not because of the physical pain I encountered with Mr. and Mrs. Langamen's children, but as a child, it was tragic being away from your friends and family. I could not stop crying until I got to my destination of about fifteen kilometers. I suffered and was confused about what was going on in my life just to pursue and be educated. However, my goal was solid and enforced. I would sacrifice all the physical pain of pinches and punches, but my mind was fixed on continuing to pursue my education. Physical pain was ignored.

My first assignment was to wash clothes at the river while the children were in school, and Mrs. Langamen watched the youngest temporarily while I was washing clothes in the river. I brought the basin full of dirty clothes, and I must put it on top of my head. I situated myself on two big rocks, able to pound clothes to wash with a paddle. At that time, there was no washing machine or dryer. This is the countryside of living, and we always go to the river to wash clothes. We would paddle the clothes against the stone. A flat paddle shaped like an oval ping pong paddle with a handle. I was only 14 years old, that year was 1971.

After my two months of work, I went home to visit my family, but I felt like I was not welcome. It seemed like my sisters ignored my coming home. I was sad that day and went back to Langamen's house to continue my responsibilities while they were paying for my High School education. One day, I met my mother on the road while walking fifteen kilometers back to Langamen's home. My mother was a beautician, and she came from her customer's house that day. I met her on the road walking back home while I was walking back to my babysitting work.

My mother saw the tears from my eyes down to my cheek, and she asked why I was crying. I told her about my older sister's attitude towards me coming home. My older sister told me not to come back home because I was not welcome anymore at my parents' house. It breaks my heart that just recently when I was in my 50s, my sister asked forgiveness to me for this incident when we were very young, at age 14 years old and my sister was 16 years old. We are now in our 60s. That's how long the realization of our action hurts someone, whether your sisters, brothers, or friends.

However, at that moment, I have forgiven my sister since, within my heart and mind, that forgiveness has given me peace of mind all along in my life journey. When forgiving someone for what they did to me that hurt my feelings, it pleases my soul and spirit. I then feel peace of mind. In my 60s, I still carry on with this type of behavior because it gives me *freedom*.

Of course, I have always forgiven my sister since we were

young until this very moment. In fact, I put her children to school instead before she asked for forgiveness in 2016. However, in the middle of putting my money into my nieces and nephews' education while I was pursuing my higher education to become a PhDs. in the USA, one of my nieces got pregnant without getting married, which was very disturbing to me. I stopped all the monetary support to all my nieces and nephews. Although the oldest niece had finished her RN degree, and the rest were almost done, only 1 or 2 subjects to be taken and then to graduate. Today, I am very conscious of giving support to anyone who does not validate the graces and blessings of what they were given and received.

Until these days, I always have a thankfulness for what I received. I am thankful that I accumulated real estate investments, sold some, and used the money to pay my previous husband's funeral expenses and other bills after the Sally Hurricane flood havoc on our living situation in September 2020. I am also thankful that we survived the flooding surge water so quickly that year. Although my previous husband, Thomas, passed away in December 2020, I again struggled to grieve his passing. I somehow always survived one at a time, just like when I almost drowned in Kawasan, the waterfall on Bohol Island, at age 10. I have survived and accumulated many skills to survive somehow.

Our journey here on earth is like a river flowing through moving forward; wishes, goals, and plans continue even in re-opening my businesses after COVID, flood, sickness, and death havoc my life. Also, when I was in my sixty's, I continued my own career as a book writer, fine art teacher, and Notary Public, and planning to re-open my limousine business here in Panama City, Florida. I completely agree that one of these businesses will not survive, but it could be a blessing if not reopened.

In the 1970s, my sister Annie was living in Manila. I did follow my sister Annie, whom I got along with most of the time when we were young. Therefore, I felt like I was guided by my conscience and wisdom to come to Manila to continue my education. I did. When I was in Manila, many things happened that I was not expecting but accepted with full heart, but awareness must be within me. I was looking for a job so I could continue my education again. I ended up with a group of people which I am not aware of. However, before this happened, my conscious mind was telling me something about this group of people. I did remember when I was 12 years old, before coming to follow my sister Annie in Manila, I ended up with the same group; it seemed was the same illegal organization. I was aware of these types of groups through my conscience and wisdom. This group of people today is called the "*Human Trafficking*."

Today, my highest education is a Doctor of Philosophy (PhDs) I earned in my 50s majoring in Human Services; I am now able to see this hidden type of activity of organizations of human trafficking, selling or exchanging workers for monetary needs of parents or organizations looking for saleable human beings, which now we call "Human Trafficking." I then became a volunteer of the Guardian Ad Litem program protecting the abused and neglected children in America. Through my own experience when I was growing up, I made a poem while I was taking my education taking Literature Art and Photography an Associate of Art (AA) degree and wrote poems in the year 1997 in the USA. Writing down my experiences when I was young was a healing process for me. In my writing assignment, I had to write an essay, and I chose this story of mine from when I was young. My essay titled The Runaway Girl was my escape from my previous scary life experience.

CHAPTER SIX

The Runaway Girl: Naivety Of A Child

The city is a jungle where I was frightened to stay. As a twelve-year-old naive girl, I feared that every animal would chase my innocent beauty. From the corner of the obscure island, one of the places in the global region, as a little girl, I had been living with five sisters, a mother as the breadwinner, and a paralyzed father. As a little girl, I was told that my duty was to help my family to survive and provide basic household necessities. However, I was deprived of family unity. Sometimes, I exclaimed! "Why me...Why me!" I exhaled and cried like an echo in the mountain where only the lions could understand my plea. I prayed, "Lord, please don't bring me to the city!" I didn't want to leave my town, and at the same time, I worried about being away from my family and friends.

I would hide my hands behind my back, which is a sign of nervousness, and try to fight back to run away from the agent who would take me to the city to look for a job so my family could be provided with basic household necessities. Tears in my eyes, and I face the ground with my bent left leg, toe up, and right leg, toe down; I squat on the ground, screaming, "Please leave me alone!" I sobbed and covered my face with my two little palms. Instead, the agents forcefully dragged me and lifted me up from the ground. The brown-colored van waited for me to be shifted to where the job in the city could be found. While the agents and my mother were busy negotiating my salary to work in the city, I was trying to get out of the brown-colored van, and I ran away and ran.

"Run! Run! Run! Away, little girl!" I said while running. "Protect yourself from these agents!" I said to myself. The only place where I could hide was the old farm. Running through the bushes, taller than I was, I made sure nobody could see my head, and I bent while looking for a place to rest. I placed myself in the bushes, covered with dried banana leaves. Tears in my eyes were still fresh until I fell asleep where the banana leaves a comfortable bed I had made. I was tired of running, which made me sleep tightly that night. At that moment, I had peace of mind there in the middle of the thick bushes that nobody could find.

After three days of being reported missing and living at my father's old farm, I came home and hid in the crawl space underneath the kitchen bamboo floor, where I found a hole to keep an eye on what was going on. I squatted on the dirty ground with my palms together placed between my knees and arms on my thighs, head down. I was afraid, and I cried silently, making sure nobody heard my breathing and crying. I looked through the hole while my sisters ate supper. I was starving, but I must wait. I waited and waited until they finished eating supper. I got up and went inside the kitchen to fill in my hunger. Because of hunger, I didn't notice that behind me was my mother. "Here she is!" my mother exclaimed. She was happy that her goal for me would be accomplished. There was no way out of my situation, only to follow without hesitation. "You must help me; your father is paralyzed. You must earn money to help me." My mother begged and released her plea.

My silent response to my mother meant that it was okay to please her plea. My mother then rearranged the schedule and called the agents outside, waiting to take me to the city. "Which one among the three daughters of yours is going with me? The agents asked. "Uhmmmmm. Where is she? Come out of there! Stop hiding from us! Because sooner or later, ahh, here comes the bus! So be ready, and besides, I already have the money for your mother, and you must be ready to go with us to the city. So, better not run away this time, did you hear? Where are you?"

The other agent was trying to scare me while I was in the attic, hiding and listening to what they were saying, and I was shivering and scared where the agents found me anyway, but the plan must be done, they said. The agents were strangers to me, so my plan was to get away from these unfamiliar people. However, it seemed like a nightmare; I felt like I was stuck and couldn't run anywhere! After, I heard my mother's cry, and I felt so bad, and the tears in my eyes slowly dragged my two legs from where in the attic I hid. I faced the agents head-on and wiped my tears behind the palm of my left hand.

My long, black, shiny, messy hair and eyes were puffy, and I was breathing hard through my nose. However, I felt like I had managed it anyway. I picked up my bag with clothes that my mother packed for me that first day of the attempted trip with the agents, who anxiously and impatiently waited. I went ahead to the edge of the road to wait for the bus going to the city. I wanted to say goodbye to all my sisters, but it seemed it was a dream because all my sisters were just busy playing while I was on the bus to be taken to the city. My hands were full of carrying my luggage, and wiping my tears was difficult. Leaning my head to the right shoulder while staring at my 3 sisters playing with their friends was a sad moment.

My long black hair swayed and was blown by the wind; I kept holding it tightly, and my right hand was unable to wave to my sisters for the last time. Voice faded, almost no sound, but words I won't forget to say, "Goodbye! Goodbye to all of you! I love you anyway. Good-bye! Goodbye! to all." Once my hands were free, I waved to all, but it seemed like my sisters never saw my tears. I sat in the rear of the bus where the mirror was so I could see through just to say one more goodbye to all. With my palm open, leaning on the glass window, slowly sliding down-- down-- down-- and down—as my head went down--down--to my seat until I could only see the dust behind the bus.

I crossed my arms together with my legs up on the seat and my head on my knees, and I closed my eyes one more time. I was tired of crying since then, I was still saying, "Good-bye sisters! Good-bye!" My lips whispered, and one single tear dropped from my eye. The tear I wiped behind my palm, down to my cheek, I close my hands together. Until then, I woke up from two hours of sleep on the bus. I looked around--passengers next to me left too fast. I was wondering where they went and what they did! Why am I still here? Others disappeared? The full bus had only five passengers left, me, the two agents (Waldo and Carmen), and I didn't know where they came from, of course, which included the driver, who became six passengers altogether.

The people are not talking to each other. I didn't hear them asking questions. I can only see them staring outside the bus window, far away, without blinking. I only heard vividly the bus engine pulling up the hill and pressing the clutch shifting. I looked at the buildings and stores and watched people go by while the bus driver tried to park nearby. "Where am I?" I questioned. "You are in the city, honey," Carmen, the agent replied. "What are we doing here?" I asked. "Well, you will stay in our house for tonight, and we will be going to the big city tomorrow, and I want you to dress up nice." Carmen gazed and smiled. "Come on! Little girl, don't worry, Carmen said. This little girl will be staying with us tonight, and my wife will take good care of you little girl. I promise I will too, said Waldo.

So long, Carmen, we'll make sure this little girl will be

happy where she temporarily stays." Waldo insisted. At the same time, Waldo's left arm is anchored to my shoulder, where I can see that he is much, much taller. He urgently, hurriedly, briskly dragged and lifted me up using my collar that my feet were elevated from the ground. "Come on, little girl, hurry up, and if you would make a big stump," he said. I was off balance walking faster but was recovered by Waldo's strong arms.

I stumbled and mumbled, and I was ready to give up. Waldo persisted, "come on sweetie, come on, don't be a slug-don't be a drag but grab your bag, hug me, whatever you do, I appreciated it anyway because I like you." Waldo laughed. Waldo's eyebrows raised with his smiling eyes which I sensed something was going on in his mind. Before someone else gets a chance; he better does it first, so they only have the second hand. Finally, after fifteen minutes of walking, Waldo and I came to the destination where I would be spending two nights before going to the big city to get a job. I was introduced to his wife, Minnie. I thought Minnie was his children's nanny. Minnie, my wife, will take good care of you little girl." Waldo said. "Little girl--- to work in the big city-- are you ready?" Ask Minnie.

I did not answer her question because I knew I was not ready. However, I thought I had found someone to talk to and to perhaps save me from this situation I am in. "You seemed to be nicer than anyone else I spoke to. Maybe I could talk to you. How I feel in all these situations, first, I do not know where to go. Second, why I am here, I thought I'd be your children's baby-sitter." I spoke. "Did you know that your mom took money from Waldo to pay expenses in your household? Since that your mom advances some money from Waldo, you'll have to pay for it by working in the big city." Minnie explained. "In the big city? What am I going to do there? in the big city?" I naively asked. "Uhmmm, maybe working with someone, like cleaning or I don't know yet." Minnie was puzzled too. In the next morning I woke up with the loud noise I heard from the other bedroom. I was curious and I put my left ear into the wall and listened to what was going on in the other room. I heard conversation with anger, fights, growls, and cries.

"How old is this kid you are bringing to the big city? And she doesn't even know where she is going to be. Haaa!, Waldo! Answer me, -- right now! -- Minnie screamed at Waldo, and it seemed he punched Waldo in the cheek. My left ear on the wall, listening to their conversation, I can sense that my life is in danger. I cried but must cry silently. To continue listening, I made sure that no one could hear me crying so I could listen more to what was going on. I heard arguments of two people, Minnie and Waldo. "She is only twelve years old, what's wrong with you!" "So, what! She is all right! Okay? Don't worry!" Waldo exclaimed. "What do you mean, don't worry. I must worry! She is just a child! Are you crazy!" Minnie was very angry. Waldo said, "Money, money,

Minnie, that drives me crazy!

"They gave me half of the payment already. The clothes you wore at the party last week, the money came from that pay, don't you know that! The jewelry you were wearing came from that money. Don't ever ruin my plan, Minnie! Because you know what's going to happen to you! Did you hear me? Hmmmm?" Waldo said to Minnie, "Stop it! Stop pulling my hair, you creep! Stay away from me!" I am out of this trouble, and you handle it by yourself because I will not be with you when the sentence comes through. You will be alone in this situation since that you haven't learned from the past!" Minnie said angrily. I heard punches and physical fights. Seems I heard sniffing, cries, confusion, and tears with this conversation. I could imagine what was going on based on what I've heard from the other room.

I thought I had a pretty good idea on what was going on! I am now ready for any time what would happen to me. I said to myself that I am the one who is responsible to myself and nobody else. So, I drew up a plan to escape. I have one more day left to stay in Waldo and Minnie's house based on what I've heard. Then, I will be shifted to the big city where the job is waiting for me. I couldn't sleep that night. I was sitting in that room by myself all night long. In the right corner I sit, chin on my knees with arms wrapped around my legs thinking in the dark I can't help crying and wept silently. I braced myself by getting ready with my bag nearby, and ready what's next.

Suddenly, the door slowly opened. Iiiick! Iiiick! Iiiick! Click! Shhhh! Quiiiite! I am here to save you, (very low voice) I want you to get out of here and save your life. Go, go, go, go, before Waldo will kill me for doing this!" It was Minnie who saved me from Waldo's hand, and I asked myself if I could survive in the city where I do not know anyone and I am not familiar with the place. "Don't forget your bag, honey," And be careful, okay?" Minnie said. I ran through the doorway and felt so free! I ran and ran to save my life, I didn't even know where I was going, whether to left or to right. I just ran.

However, I said to myself to think quickly and decide where to go. In my thoughts I remembered my father's farm where I could see and feel fresh air and it was so peaceful and calm. I said that maybe in the forest where all the green trees and fresh air and smells of newly cut grass up hills would give me peace of mind. While running I was thinking that perhaps, in the city where all cars and people can see me that I need help. I was confused, and I thought in the middle of the road cars would come and go after me. The hiding sunrise peeping in the morning and to me it seems the sunrays were playing with me behind trees.

In comparison, in the evening the city sleeps late at night I have witnessed the buzzing, whistling, lights low and high beam lights blinking. Meanwhile, in the forest I could move my legs and run free. I could hear the birds singing perched on the branch of the tree. In the city is like a jungle, I could only hear engines running all over and near me. I inhaled dusty road I didn't recognize that those are not fresh air. My arms shifting left and right walking running and walking fast, I sometimes my arm I would place it on my forehead to protect my eyes from damaging bright light at night. I would get out from the middle of the road and move on to the side, but I only struggled to protect myself from people's humiliation.

The car drivers were screaming, spitting, clapping, laughing, and cheering on me and said, "Poor little girl full of embarrassment"! I tried to stay away from the needy greedy on the road. I stand straight to be ready for my right of way to escape and from these activities of car fights. "Screeeech! Stop! Hold!" These were all what I've heard. "Excuse me, oppsss, stoppp, holddd onnn, thank you sir." My both hands pushed toward the hood of the car to protect myself from being on a head on collision. Going through the traffic in the city for me was dangerous and devastating. I patiently wait for someone to help.

I rested and sat in the corner so people could see me. People just passed through me and perhaps they thought that I needed some money. I watched people go by dropping coins in front of me. I watched the coins drop on my head. I felt the coins dropped on my head rolling towards my face; I saw the coins ups and downs while watching the coins fall on the ground. I picked it up and gave it back to that person of the given money I don't need. What I really need is someone to talk to. So, I returned these monies they were dropping in front of me. I said, "No, thank you sir, I don't need money!" No, thank you ma'am, I don't need it." I would shake my head to make sure that they understand me that I do not need the money, but I need someone to talk to.

I changed my strategy, and I walked along the stores and asked what bus will pass by to go to my hometown. People said, "What are you doing in downtown little girl--this late at night? I would avoid answering that question because my situation was too complicated. I, myself, do not understand what was going on. What I know was that I ran away, and Minnie helped me to escape.

The night was so nasty, rainy, foggy, and dew were in the air of the city. I walked along the side of the road and found an abandoned shed with a hole in the roof. I sat down waiting for the rain to stop. Someone was coming to where I was which I felt like the danger was just right there. I quickly hid in the back of the shed. The back of the shed was surrounded with grass and bushes, it was dark, and there were too many dried leaves and broken branches. I took one of my biggest towels from my bag to protect myself from the nasty weather I encountered that night behind the shed.

The drunken passersby saw the abandoned shed. The two

also needed shelter from the nasty weather. "Come on, let's sit down for a while, I am very tired walking from the city. Man, I have a headache, man." the drunkard complained. "Man, let us pass the night in the shed and wait for the rain to calm down a little bit." The other drunkard exhaled. The two drunkards waited until the rain drifted. They heard something crisping in the back of the shed. They looked around to see if there was someone to witness what they did. The drunkard was almost on the edge to see me hiding comfortably with all the bushes and twigs in the back of the shed. I slowly lifted my foot not to step on those dried small branches to only make noise.

Luckily, the blue towel I was using is like the color of the night and the surroundings. The conversation I heard was like an echo of the danger in this shelter shed. Whimpering with fear, I hid silently when the drunkards were about to leave. I was left behind and I made sure they had completely disappeared. I went back inside the shed and made it comfortable on the bench bed. I slept until the crickets woke me up and birds sang me a lovely morning song. "Excuse me, I am lost, please help me." Ahmm-- Ahmm--I am from, ahmm, three towns from here, so, I would like to go home, ahmm-- ahmm-- would you help me please?" I honestly insisted. The next van stopped by the shed and asked if I needed help. I answered the big yes. However, there were 3 men inside the van. In the beginning it looks like they are nice people.

Someone was interested in helping me and guided me

through where I must go. I was in the van full asleep for a long time and woke up and felt like I was lost again. It seems I am in a different place. The place was so unfamiliar. The place when I woke up was like the parking of an airplane. While we were all in the car, that used to be a van, I was puzzled. "Honey, this is now your hometown and city, remember?" Are we still on Bohol Island? I asked? "No. Honey, come follow me," the van driver said. Where are we? I asked. "We are now in Manila?" The van driver said. "We are in Manila?" I was confused. The van driver continued and said to me, "I am the person who will be responsible for you." Again, I asked, "Where am I? Are they going to send me back to my hometown? "Honey, this is your hometown." "Excuse me sir--, sir--, sir--, sir-! This is not my hometown." I insisted.

Their actions were so odd. I thought and I am sure that I am in the hands of people that I should not trust. While the driver was driving the car for only an hour, the driver parked the car inside a garage, and it seemed there were so many people in this place where again I ended up. I saw inside this house so many girls my age and some were older than me. These are all young girls. I questioned myself as if what are they doing here. All of us were in a room where there were no beds, only handmade mats on the floor.

There was only one bathroom, and the kitchen was located downstairs. When it is time for dinner, all girls must fill in line, a long line. I could not answer my questions on how it happened that from Bohol Island to Manila without knowing being captured and came to the big city by ship at that time 2 days of travel? By airplane it could be so expensive, but now I am sure that I am in Manila on the other side of the island that will only take 45 minutes by airplane versus ship that takes 2 days on the sea. These are still my questions that until these days were a puzzle to me. Although I survived, questions still lingered in my mind now that I am in my 60s.

Furthermore, there must be at least 100 girls there in this house I am in that day they brought me to Manila. There must be more rooms in that house to house more than 100 girls, I thought. I discovered that there were at least 3 bedrooms in the house, now that it was a house with too many very young girls, more than 20 girls in every room. These girls, including me, would fill in line to eat breakfast and after eating we would go back to share a room with more than 20 young girls. We stood in line the cook gave each girls a bowl with some kind a gruel for breakfast. I also saw guards near the doors. The only reason I get out of the bedroom is to use the toilet. My mind is working and thinking about what is going on. My mind is puzzled and thinking why these girls are stuck here and seem to be unable to do anything to get out of the area where we sleep and eat only.

One day, I saw 2 girls were forced to be picked up and brought to the door, but the struggles seem very odd. The girls disagree but can't fight with 2 strong men dragging them out the door and car is waiting for these 2 young girls. I put all the puzzles and connect the pieces of what's going on. I can see and feel that this is another Waldo and Carmen's recruitment of young girls in the island where I was born. I then created a strategy on how to get out of the house with 100 young girls. I asked four young girls to escape with me up the window nearby. Two young girls refused to escape and were very distraught and seemed very scared. I saw her neck had bruises. Both girls refused to escape, and the other 2 girls escaped with me. I climbed up the window one night and 2 young girls came with me, and we ran and ran faster until we got to the place where we thought it was safe. It seems it was easy to run away but courage, strength and faith must accompany our plan. Three of us ended up in town where we could find a job to survive. We found a waitressing job in the town of Tondo.

As young as we are we were accepted to serve in the restaurant that sometimes we must examine who we are serving, it could be that we will be back in that house with 100 young girls cornered. I was very right that one day I saw these 2 guys who guarded us in that house with 100 young girls cornered, and I told my 2 friends that we must run away as soon as possible. Only 2 days of that restaurant working at least we got little money from tips while serving. Therefore, we were able to again run away farther from that place with 100 young girls cornered. My friends and I found another restaurant to be employed farther away from that house with 100 young girls and we were so happy that we were accepted in that restaurant for a waitressing job. Even in these days of my age of 60s I am still very careful who I meet. I can only trust someone that I am able to see respectful behavior and have a good heart. I developed an aloof behavior that made me distant from what I think is a danger zone.

There are times I stayed away from someone who I can feel and smell a danger lurking around the corner. I am very distrustful that my life became so distant to something or someone who I can feel not safe to be with. However, through my education in a higher level as a Doctor of Philosophy (PhDs) studied human behavior as majored in Human Services, I learned how people think, developed life pattern, and inherited behavior from what they have been experienced while growing up. I was able to examine who they are and determine a situation and decision between those analysis. I would ask the question if they have learned from what had happened to them while growing up. Were they able to manage themselves to realign their lives from disastrous experiences in life? Those questions I asked I also learned on how to manage myself in disastrous type of life, the aloofness I have learned that comes to me anytime of my life. I then learned in my study and research the experiences of humanity, especially young girls, like what had happened to me while growing up. Therefore, I now understand.

Through their answers, I can figure out who they were and

are and what they are capable of. I am thankful for the higher education I have accomplished. The goals I have accomplished to be educated since I was 12 years old, now in my 60s, are truly appreciated and worth it. I am thankful that I came here in the USA. I am and was grateful to my husband at that time, to whom I married, Thomas, for 22 years since 1997, who passed away on December 17, 2020, as my encourager to continue my education to a higher level. I then fulfilled my dream come true in higher education, and now I am a Doctor of Philosophy graduate in the year 2014 at Capella University. Thomas was my confidante while pursuing my education to a higher level. Thomas is now with the Lord, and wherever you are, my dear, you are truly appreciated.

To continue the story of when I was young, I remember after escaping and running away from the house with more than 100 girls trapped, I was able to find a job. I was earning more income at age 15 to 16 years old. My pursuit of higher education was fulfilled because of my intention to do so with persistence, dedication, focus, and positive motivation. Then, I accomplished my goals in life despite the hardships and struggles I have encountered.

Another experience I've been through when I was young, I was employed as a dog sitter in the big city, I again encountered predator which I could not tell at the time of who they were within their hearts and minds and unknowledgeable to their behavior at that time while I was very young, I became the prey.

THE MEMOIR: THE RIVER OF LIFE

CHAPTER SEVEN

The Mansion: Danger Is On The Way

When I was 16 to 17 years of age, I used to take care of 3 little poodles. Their names are Puppet, Honey, and Santa Clause. While I was seeking jobs in Manila, I found a job to take care of small little poodles. The house I was living in was a mansion. The retired couple who lives in this mansion are Mr. Tapia, a retired Engineer, and his wife, Dr. Tapia, a retired medical doctor. They have two daughters. One was a teacher, and the youngest was an attorney. Both daughters are married. However, the daughter, who was a teacher, lived separately with 2 children, and the youngest one with her husband lived in the mansion. Mr. and Dr. Tapia's youngest daughter has 3 poodles that need me to take care of these 3 lovely little dogs.

This mansion was a beautiful home that was always chosen by filmmakers to make movies because movie makers would rent this mansion for filming. This family has a driver, maids, and dog sitter, me. While taking care of these 3 beautiful little poodles, I would watch the movie makers filming, and sometimes they needed extra character, and I was always there. It was a different life I have been through, but it was a little pride that came with it. It is like Hollywood characters in the movie here in the USA. While working with a retired couple as a dog sitter, I was enjoying the place and the privileges that come with it. Such are those riding in a Mercedes Benz with the driver wearing a uniform once I needed food to go to the grocery for my Poodles.

The Mansion was a place for filmmakers to rent the whole huge, beautiful property for movies. I was once used as a caretaker of the house in the film. If I could remember, the title of the movie was "The Flying Salakot." I am not sure if that's the right spelling of the movie title "Salakot." My character was to point out the person who was asking for someone and in what bedroom he was waiting for this guest. It was an amazing experience to be part of the filming, but there was something in the air. I could smell the danger lurking while working for this couple at the Mansion.

However, all I do with that responsibility as a dog sitter is to make sure the Poodles are vaccinated and taking vitamins just like humans. There were times when only Mr. Tapia and I were left in the house. The maids are either going to groceries or assisting Dr. Tapia to go shopping as an assistant. I respect Mr. Tapia, just like my grandfather or maybe my great-grandpa. While Mr. Tapia was fixing something up in the attic, I was busy feeding my beautiful 3 little poodles. Mr. Tapia called me while he was in the attic to bring something for him, a hammer.

I followed his instructions on where to get the hammer. He said to go to the garage, and on the left shelf of the tools area, I will find a hammer. I did what he instructed me. I found the hammer easy. I brought the hammer to him. While on the floor, I look at him in the attic hole. I see the long ladder to climb up to the attic. He instructed me to come to the attic through the ladder. I was a little hesitant because the ladder was very high. I started climbing, but I went back down. I said to Mr. Tapia that I couldn't do it if he could wait for the driver to give that hammer to him. He insisted on bringing the hammer to him and was a little aggravated. With his guidance on how to climb up, I was forced to climb up to bring the hammer to him up in the attic.

Again, using my common sense and wisdom, his purpose was not the need for the hammer. I've never thought that an eighty-year-old man, a retired engineer, would take advantage of a 17-year-old naïve little girl, a dog sitter. I still remember the place I left the house of 100 girls trapped and ran away from, and I felt I was back to this type of house but just by myself. And the house is much more decent and pleasant to live in, a huge mansion with 7 bedrooms with maids, a driver, and a dog sitter, me.

On the last step up in the attic, he grabbed me and put me in the attic with him, and Mr. Tapia started messing around with me. I was so frightened and insisted on saying the word to him *"no,"* but at the same time, I was crying and begged him to release me from his strong arm. What I did was while fighting away from him, and while he was trying to caress me, I put my two legs down on the first ladder step, then to the second step, and to the third, and tried and enforced to get off from him. Then, I bit his hands that were holding me from going down the stairs. It seems I again repeated this action, "biting" the hands.

I then pulled my body and head from his strong hands and slid down my body through the ladder steps while biting his arms and holding me up. I was using my teeth to get away from Mr. Tapia, similar to a previous event when I was 13 years old. I finally got out from him, but I fell on the floor and went to the door quickly and ran away from him while he was still in the attic. I went to the garden again and stayed there for a long time. I didn't feel the aches due to falling, but the next day, I was in pain. I was in the garden resting and reminiscing about the past because this type of incident is like what had happened to me babysitting for this couple who were teachers in the community. It was a similar incident.

I told one of the maids about that action of Mr. Tapia. After a month, I requested to look for another job. My reasoning was that I must be near my sister Annie, where she lives. I did. After leaving that Mansion, I still have a connection with the rest of the maids. I spoke to one of the maids, and she left the Mansion because she got pregnant by Mr. Tapia, and the wife, Dr. Tapia, found out. Therefore, the maid who got pregnant was fired. I came to realize that it is truly helpful to just *run away*. Avoid this type of circumstance and be vigilant. I then learned to be "vigilant."

When you smell and feel the danger, get ready and just run away from it. I was thankful to the Lord that since then, the Lord has always been with me until these days. The Lord is always giving me the feeling of common sense and wisdom that I used and still use these days to make sense of any type of incident on what's going on around us. I am thankful to the Lord that He is giving me the skills of good common sense, good wisdom, and good conscience. Thank you, Lord. Amen. I am saved.

CHAPTER EIGHT

Fire At Kagitingan Street: Faith Is a Decision

In the year 1975, I was 18 years of age; I was already managing a restaurant. From where I worked, I could see the top roof where I lived. I live with my sister Annie and her three-month-old baby boy; we call him First Nephew. I was working and training employees on the second floor of the restaurant; I saw lots of people on the road looking towards where I live. So, I came down and looked. I saw smoke. A big thick smoke around where I lived. My sister Annie was assigned to the town of Isabela at that time as her work required her to go companies to company as a security guard. She was a security guard in one of the companies there. So, I asked one of my co-workers to take care of the restaurant while I was heading home and see what was going on. "Manang, I need to go home to see what's going on," I said. "Sure, sure. Go! Go! I looked for a taxi to take me there.

I couldn't find one, so I ran and ran to get to where the smoke came from. I went to my sister's apartment, where I lived temporarily. On the second floor, the apartments there were close to each other. I usually called an apartment to sound nice, but it was a place where squatters lived. The area was a slum. My sister lived in a slum house like the favela in Brazil, which I wrote a paper on when I was in my undergrad at Brookdale Community College in

New Jersey, continuing my education from 1995 to 1997.

At my sister Annie's apartment, she was living in the upper section. There was stinky water along the pathway. There were mosquitoes. You can hear people coughing at each other. The clothes they were wearing were the same for the whole month. You could smell them, and you could throw up. This was how they lived. Only my sister was a little bit decent. I asked my sister one day why she was living in this kind of location. "The rent was cheap, and I could get some help to watch my baby if I am assigned to faraway places," she said. The houses were slanted. It looked like they were falling into one another's house. The backyards were filthy. There were hundreds of hundreds of metal tubes piled to one another. Inside the metal tube was trash, like papers, cartons, and other things. On the side of every pile, there was human waste, and it smelled every time the wind went to my sister's apartment. I was living there because I worked nearby.

I was planning to leave my sister and stay somewhere clean and in nice surroundings. Suddenly, I heard shouting, "Fire! Fire! Everyone shouted. I looked around and found a suitcase and packed all my clothes and my sister's clothes. I dropped it in the backyard, where all these piles of metals and tubes were located. "Fire! Fire! Everyone shouted again. After putting all the important things in, I went downstairs to drag all the things I dropped from the second floor. The fire was trying to catch me. I assumed. There were gasoline cans floating in the air and exploded. I was trying to avoid those things flying up in the air.

The explosion of some houses nearby was very loud, and fire scattered all over. Everyone was screaming and running. While I was dragging all the luggage and other things, I was almost at the end of the roadside, and I remembered my nephew downstairs with the babysitter. I put all the things I rescued and went back to the house. The police had already made a blockade in the area. I begged them for me to come inside because my nephew, First Nephew, was still there inside. I must rescue my nephew, my three-month-old nephew. "Please let me in. My nephew is inside the house. In that house. Downstairs. Please let me in." I was crying and begging. "No. You can't. You can't." a police officer said.

While the police were busy helping other people, I sneaked out and ran all the way to where my nephew was. I saw my nephew innocently sleeping in the hammock. I picked him up without cover and underwear. His face was full of ashes, burnt elements carried by the wind. I wiped it out carefully so as not to wake him up, not to see what was going on; he didn't have to know. I ran and ran all the way to the edge of the road. I cried and cried. While the police were following me and other newscasters after the fire, we stayed in an empty school. I found my picture and the baby headline the next morning. I felt like I was so ugly in that photo because my face was full of ashes, and I was crying. My face was full of ashes; you couldn't recognize me and my nephew's face.

We looked like soldiers with camouflage, with lines and streaks that split the ashes on my face when tears came down from my eyes to my cheek. On that day, I was looking for the babysitter, and I'd like to ask questions about why she left my nephew in the hammock and she ran away with her child. At the same time, she was also looking for me at that facility. They found me through the newspaper, where my nephew and I were featured on the front page. I would like to ask her why she left my nephew by himself in the hammock. Why? They found me where all the fire victims were located. "I need to get the baby back," the babysitter told me. "For what? You left my nephew unattended, and then you want him back? For what? I angrily asked. "Your sister didn't pay me for how many months, so I need to have her baby." The babysitter said. "No. You can't have the baby." I insisted. "You can't feed and take good care of my nephew. I was going to call the police to arrest the babysitter for neglecting my nephew, but I changed my mind because she also had a daughter with her. It's going to be complicated.

However, the babysitter insisted on getting back my nephew. She said that he had all the tools to take care of my nephew, but I argued with her. "I have all the tools, and I know how to take care of him." the babysitter insisted. I responded, "No, I will go to my work, and they will help me." I insisted. After two months as one of the victims of that fire from Kagitingan, I finally realigned, moved, and transferred my nephew to my parents, away from that Favela house my sister was living in.

Heading to my parents' house away from that, Favela took 2 days on a ship to travel on the sea. My nephew was well taken care of in Bohol Island, the smallest island where I was born. My First Nephew is now in his 30s. I put him to school while I was in the USA from year 1984 to these days. He graduated and is now working with the municipality in my childhood hometown. To continue my memoir of the river of life in the year 1975 in Manila, my life changed dramatically. However, there are many unexplainable reasons why MyFirstNephew hates me so much for saving his life from the fire and not appreciating what has been given to him because it's not enough. A person who is not grateful for life and not thankful for the blessing given will go through hardship in life again due to many misunderstandings of blessings and abundance given by the Lord. Little blessings and abundance have been given, and its thankfulness will always be the guidance of seeing and getting more blessings in a spiritual world of understanding the Almighty's gifts to humanity.

Unable to acknowledge these gifts from the Almighty creates a barrier to moving forward in life, but instead, it would develop hatred, negativity, worry, and selfishness. Therefore, struggles and unpleasant living style occurs. I invite you to read my

Two Universes of Self Part 2: The Thought Universe, which will soon be published. This book will explain our thinking that becomes the place to gather previous experiences and life activities and become the luggage in mind or, shall I say, a cargo that prevents us from being thankful and vice versa. Hate, worries, stress, and bad experiences in life bring us to the negativity that ruins more of our thoughts, taking away from the goodness of life that we are supposed to have here on earth. The Lord has already given us this freedom, but we need to acknowledge it and see the good things that He has given to us all. Thankfulness can bring you to the other side of the world, the fruitful life, while passing through this earth of plenty.

I have been managing my businesses since 2004 in Art, Notary Public, rental properties, and as a mortgage signing agent since 1998 to these days, and as my life experiences since when I was young. Living here in the USA and pursuing my education at a higher level, I graduated in 2014 from a doctoral program specializing in Management and Leadership in Human Services. At the same time, I volunteered at the Guardian Ad Litem Program to be a licensed Court Officer to protect and be the voice of neglected and abused children. I also attended a court hearing to fight for neglected and abused children in three counties.

I visited families with issues in filing custody, a battle for husband, wife, and family members. I fight for children who are prescribed too many medications. Due to too many medications, these children are becoming like zombies. Attending a meeting with teachers and parents to let them know, and with agreements from the team, I saved a child by removing four types of medications from 7 all the total medications taken. Reminiscing about life experiences and learning from our mistakes enables us to move forward in life, choosing the road to the right path.

CHAPTER NINE

The Captive: Living A Luxurious Life

Starting from the year of 1979, my life changed in a different direction. It was the four corners I always encountered. There was one eleven-inch colored television in the corner on the right side near my bed. The cassette tape was always on for listening to music. Trying to kill the time and forget the clock ticking. My room was sealed like a cocoon. The metal window surrounding me was solid like a rock. I can't move. I can't exhale. I can't decide for myself. I can't even think of my own. The Guard was after me whenever I acted suspiciously. If I acted to escape, the guard was there for me to arrest and put it back where I could only see the four corners of my room like I was in jail. That's how I felt where I was at that moment of my life.

Before I do anything for myself, like watching a movie, going shopping, going to the mall, or even enjoying nature outside, I must think first before even acting and follow my self-gratification. If I decide on my own, I feel like I will be punished by staying inside my room for a week, which I call jail. I will be punished by means of suffering my life out there in the crowd of people looking for jobs and wanting to survive in life. Would I stay in my present surroundings with everything I needed with a guard and driver on my side, two maids watching what I am doing, and maids doing things for me? Weekly financial allowance that satisfies my world needs. However, I am feeling cornered and captive. Which one should I choose? Should I choose freedom or a material and financially abundant lifestyle?

I was once considered financially able to help my parents when I was 11 years of age. I sell fish in my neighborhood. My mother and I would go to the sea, where fishermen sell fish wholesale. I would put these fish in a basket and use a towel to set the basket full of fish on my head. I then started walking from house to house to sell fish in my neighborhood. Although I just go along with the flow of life, I came from a very poor family after my father was sick. We didn't have television in comparison to these days. My mother was a beautician and a live performing artist, such as a drama and singing performer. My father was a photographer but was paralyzed after falling from a coconut tree. Everything in my mother's world crumbles.

While growing up, at age 15, the only action I could take to improve my life was to meet a rich man; that became a practice for young ladies at that time of my life. To support the family's needs and my needs, which most girls or ladies consider a dream come true. But I didn't really think about that as my priority in life. My priority is to educate myself to a higher level of education. However, at that moment of chaos and wish to help my parents, I just wish to have this kind of person in my life so that I will be free of responsibility for providing monetary needs for my family. Since I was twelve years old, I have been working just to survive and help my family. There are times when I would quit providing monetary support for my family and just think about my own needs. But it was difficult, and I felt guilty at that moment, unable to help my parents regarding financial support.

One day, I went to a big city and got lost. I was by myself. I stayed near the theatre to be safe from other unscrupulous people in the city. I went to different bazaars to look for a job. One bazaar accepted me, and I started work immediately. The owner of the bazaar was a Chinese man living by himself. I was a stock girl. I went to the attic and dropped some toys for the customer's order down to the store using a dump waiter, we called it. I stayed there until my boss called me to come down and help in the store. After my duty in the attic, I would go to my employer's house to sleep. I was a live-in employee. This means living in the employer's house free of rent.

My boss would scream and yell at me, saying to bring my mat and sit to sleep near the bathroom. "Yes, sir." In my feared sound. I forgot something after I came down the stairs, and I went back up again. I asked my boss, "Sir, I forgot where my portable bed is located; where is it, sir.?" I asked. "Go downstairs, and you will see it under the stairs." the boss replied. I was looking for the bed downstairs, but I couldn't find it. I went back up again and asked my boss. "Sir, I couldn't find the portable bed, sir?" I asked again. "It is downstairs! My boss said with annoyance in his voice. "Those open boxes downstairs are your portable bed." First, I stared at those boxes and shook my head. I opened empty boxes and made it into my bed, realigning near the bathroom door as my boss said.

My boss's voice seemed angry, and I ran downstairs nervously and picked up the open boxes as my portable bed opened it wide to fit me. I never bothered my boss for a blanket. I slept on the opened box without a blanket. I curled my body to get warmth, and my pillow was my bag of clothes. My boss came down to use the bathroom and screamed at me to move because he had to open the door of the bathroom to use it. My boss would kick me to move to the other side of the bathroom. "Move to the side. You are blocking the bathroom! Stupid!" the boss said. "Sir, can I spread my boxes near the dining table? I think there is a little room there," I begged. My boss said a big "No.

The table has many things on top, like those big boxes, he said. These big boxes might fall on you." the boss replied. The next morning, I woke up early and worked in the attic where toys were stored. I arrange toys and put them in order. "Toys, so many toys. I wish they were mine." I whispered. My boss heard me talking to myself. I was playing upstairs while arranging all the toys, and of course, I played with the toys, and my boss was screaming to stop jumping. My boss asked "what are you doing up there? Are you talking to someone?" my boss asked. "Oh! No. No, sir. I was just arranging all the toys and putting them in the right boxes." I replied.

After two weeks of working, I got sick, and I had to leave the bazaar because my boss couldn't afford to pay a sick worker. He kicked me out of the bazaar. I then had to go somewhere which I didn't know where to go. I then stayed and slept for many days and nights in the theatre where I stood the first time I came to a big city from my small hometown, at the doorstep on the right side of the theatre door where I situated myself to sleep for that night. The next day, I woke up early and browsed around the city looking for a job. I found a job as a waitress near the theatre. After many days of working as a waitress, I found an apartment that had room for rent. There were many tenants in this apartment with rooms for rent. We share a bath and kitchen.

I found a new job nearby as a waitress, and I felt settled. However, the rent was too expensive, so I needed to have another job. While being a waitress in the evening, I found another day job, modeling clothes. Also, taking classes in making clothes at Beauty Art School helps me to learn modeling classes and the styles of the seasons for showing. I chose to model normal wear such as party clothing, hunting clothing for that season, wedding clothes, and many other normal wear types of clothing, to specify not bikini or very body shows types of clothing. The modeling company showed me the bikini and the salary to model the skimpy bikini. The fee for modeling skimpy bikinis was higher than just an ordinary type of modeling clothes. My conscience was telling me not to model the skimpy bikini. I then accepted the modeling normal clothing such as hunting clothing for women, wedding gowns, party clothing, and many other normal wears clothing. Although the pay is almost half in comparison to skimpy bikini modeling, I accepted the normal wear modeling instead.

My first day serving as a waitress in a restaurant with a bar selling liquor was a little bit overwhelming because it was my first waitressing job experience for this type of restaurant. I had never done any waitressing job of this kind since I was waitressing and managing a restaurant with food only to serve, not liquor. After training, my first approach supposedly is greeting the customer and calling him or them "sir." "Good evening, Sir. Let me guide you to your table, sir." I asked one of the customers. "Give us some beer," the customer said. He asked me what is my name. Oh! I said Sofia, Sofia is my name, sir, "Uhmm, nice name." One of the customers replied. I showed my customer my name tag and nodded and said, "Yes sir, and thank you, sir." One of the customers had an admiration of my name, "Sofia." He continued that the meaning of Sofia's word is "Wisdom." I said, "Oh Okay."

The customer asked if I could sit down with them, all seven customers in total, at one big table. I said that I am here to work and serve; that's all I can do, sir. "I have to serve, sir," I spoke. The customer insisted and wanted to talk to the manager of the restaurant. One of the people in this group went to the Manager's office, and I saw them talking, but I could not hear what they were talking about. The manager came to me near the table I was serving, and I was very scared that I might get fired. I need this job; I said it through my imagination. The manager asked for forgiveness from the customer, who asked me to sit down with him. I was very confused. Then my manager ordered me to sit down with this man.

I found out that this man was a businessman in the area, and those men with him were his employees. I sat down with this man, and I heard their conversations about who they were. I listened and found out who they were and the man I was sitting with. Also, I found out that he had been watching me while modeling those clothes on stage in another city nearby. That night, I was a little uncomfortable. I sometimes pretend I need to use the restroom and just stay away from this group. Sometimes, I was not aware that I was just sitting there near the sink and just thinking. One of the men's men went to my manager and complained because I took so long in the restroom.

Mr. Takamoto, the manager, knocked on the restroom door, and I pretended to respond to the word "coming" and pretended I flushed the toilet, and I said, "I am coming." I did and sat with this man again. The man said, "Thank you" to my manager. Late at night, this group said goodbye, and the man was telling me he'd come back and had a plan for me. I was puzzled and nervous. I told one of my friends and co-workers, but they were just laughing, and they thought it was funny. I felt like I was ignored by my friends, and I was very frightened and thinking not to work the next night. However, I must work because I am renting a room and sending money home to my parents. I can't afford not to have a job. Now, I have two jobs: modeling clothes and waitressing at night. I feel like I can afford not to do the waitressing, but the money I send to my parents will not be enough; therefore, I continue working with my two jobs, waitressing and modeling.

The next night, I was ready to work and prepare my table for my customers as a waitress, but that night, I was in the kitchen getting things to prepare my table. I was making myself alert and kept peeping through the door to see if my previous customers were coming. This group came back and sat exactly where the table they were sitting at the other night. At 8:00 o'clock at night, this man requested for me not to serve them but to sit down with them next to the man who seemed their leader. The manager right away was looking for me.

Someone else greeted them to serve but requested me to sit with this man instead. The other waitress greeted them with respect by saying, good evening, sir" I will be serving you tonight. How can I help you sir? The man asked my name and requested for me to come to the table. The manager and the other waitress were looking for me. They found me in the kitchen looking for something and told me that Table 7 was requesting me to come and sit with them. I came and peeped through the doorhole of who they were, and of course, I knew who they were. The manager forced me to go and sit with them. In the beginning, I refused to sit with this group. I said to my manager, "I decided not to sit with this group." I said respectfully to my manager. My manager did not agree, and I feel that I will be fired. Although I am reluctant to sit with this man, I must "I guess," or I will be fired!

Anyhow, I was nervous and reluctant to sit with this group because I knew they wanted me not to serve but to sit down with this man. I remember this man told me through whispering to my ears that night they left, saying, "I have a plan for you." I will never forget that. I am very nervous and, at the same time, very anxious to know what his plan for me is. I asked one of the waitresses to watch me wherever I go. I somehow had a phobia of being treated this way. Heading to the table where they were, my mind was busy thinking and analyzing what to do. While heading to the table, I was listening to their conversation. This man seems a special man, I thought. While sitting with them, I knew that this man who wanted me to sit next to him was their boss.

I am thinking why this man has so much attention on me. I just do not understand. Through talking and trying to understand, this man has an agenda for me. For reputation purposes, we will call him BreadWinnerMan, one of the business owners of a manufacturing business in that country. He owned a big manufacturing business in a secluded town. He manufactured light bulbs, springs, and rubbers of any kind. For example, an electric fan, the rubber under to stand or to protect the table from getting scratched, and many more. He dealt with many businesspeople in that country and another country, such as China.

While sitting with him, he reached out into his pocket and took out some hundreds of paper bills from his wallet. He gave me this money, which I do not know how much. "You do not need to serve," He said. Mr. Takamoto said to BreadWinnerMan not to pay Sofia while sitting with them at their table. "Sir, no worries; Sofia can sit down with you without payment. Sir, no problem." Mr. Takamoto replied. "Oh! Sofia, here is your salary." He spoke. He handed me P21,000.00 pesos, which is worth $467.00, with 45 pesos equivalent to a dollar at that time, which was many years of my salary. I was reluctant to accept it, and I had so many questions in my mind about why he was doing this. I accept it anyway. I needed it, I said silently. I was thinking of keeping it just in case he is looking for it, and I have it in my hand to return to him. However, in my mind, I was thinking and hoping that he would not take it back.

I thought BreadWinnerMan was crazy, drunk, and hallucinating at that time. When I was working at the store bazaar, I was only earning 200.00 pesos a month ($4.45). Now, someone is giving me a big amount of money! Many years of salary! Is this true? Maybe I am just dreaming? I pinched myself. So, I got hurt by my pinch, so I am not dreaming. It's true. I look at the money, and it's true money! Then I asked myself again as if I was dreaming, maybe. Maybe he was dreaming, too, or maybe he was crazy. I was totally confused about what to do with the money.

I went to the bathroom and put the money in my handbag nervously. I came back to the table and just talked to him the whole night through. I didn't serve, and I was off that night. I am thinking, "This can't be happening. I thought. "He must be a crazy guy." There was another guy with him, and he seemed like his assistant. I asked him what his name was because he always follows BreadWinnerMan's command. He responded, "My name is Moises." The man replied.

At that moment, I was going to ask Moises why he always followed his command, but I held off on those questions because there were so many questions I wanted to ask. Moises was around fifty years old but stocky and strong. He had big muscles and a brave, deep voice, and his eyes were very sharp. Moises was BreadWinnerMan's guard and protector. Moises came from prison for a crime he committed and was sentenced to 15 years. He's been released for 6 months partly because of BreadWinnerMan's financial help. He was always there, and I had to sit down with him every night until he decided to talk to me about getting out of being a waitress. He told me that he had a plan for me. Those were his words, "I have a plan for you," that kept me awake every night thinking about what his plan for me was about.

One day, while I was modeling that day, I saw him watching me below the stage show. I didn't know that he was coming that day. I was a little bit reluctant and shy to say hello or to show him I saw him. After my modeling, he approached me to have dinner with him. I was hungry, so I agreed. We went to this very expensive restaurant called "Aristocrat Restaurant." I found out that in this restaurant, only rich people can afford to eat. This was my first time in this type of restaurant. We have our own waiter standing by. We were on the 3rd floor, and we were guarded somehow. This was the first time I ate fish eggs; we called it "caviar."

Finally, after three months of getting to know each other, he told me his plan. I must think about it first and analyze my situation at that time, living with people in a small rental apartment and sharing everything. It didn't take long; I decided to follow BreadWinnerMan's plan for me. The next day, he invited me to come with him that day, and he was going to show me the surprise he had been planning for me. "Come on, darling, I will show you the house you will be living in." The house had four bedrooms and three bathrooms, with a nice porch and backyard. He said with excitement. For me, it was a pleasure to have a house to live in, and

I didn't have to stay in the theatre and live with many tenants in a room.

Besides, I do not need to look for a job to survive and help my parents with financial hardship. I will have a decent living situation and a house. It seems a huge privilege for me. So, I agreed with the deal. I thought, just give me a house, and I will do anything you want, and I don't have to live in an apartment with so many tenants. "Darling, these are your clothes. I want you to wear these whenever I am here. I will visit you twice a week, on Tuesday and Thursday." He explained. I didn't really pay attention to these privileges given to me by this man. I said privileges because it was too extreme, and I felt like I was so lucky. I went into the house I will be living in, and it's a huge house for me to live in. I was happy and so surprised.

However, I complained because the house was too big for me, and I would be alone there. This was a big house for me to live by myself." "Well, I will get two maids for you," he said. Maids? I questioned. The master bedroom is for you and me, the other room next to the second bathroom is for the maid, and the two bedrooms are for guests" Aww! I pinched myself. Am I dreaming? I said to myself silently. I will be scared to live here, I said.

I had never lived in a big house before besides the Mansion. I used to work to take care of 3 beautiful Poodles and left due to the danger lurking around the corner for me in that Mansion. So, seems like I am back in this type of situation, so I said to BreadWinnerMan, I need time to think about it. I said, "Let me think about it first." "Oh! no, I already paid for this house." He said. "What?" I asked. "Don't worry, Mang Moises will be your guard. He has his own quarter outside near your room window." He said. My enthusiasm for having a big house changed, but I ignored the feeling of inadequacy. I felt like I was cornered. But I accepted it anyway.

The next day, BreadWinnerMan introduced me to more people I didn't know. Only Moises I knew because I met him at the restaurant. "This is Mang Moises, you know him. Moises is your guard and driver. Nori is your maid to do your laundry, cooking, and cleaning, He continued. "Hello, Ma'am Sofia," Mang Moises and Nori greeted me like I was a queen or a princess with a head vow. Is this really happening to me? I asked myself that question.

That was a very different type of lifestyle for me. Never had that before. I was the one who vowed and said the greetings of yes sir or yes ma'am. Mang Moises nodded, and Nori vowed to me. I was very uncomfortable calling me the word "ma'am." I am living in a 4-bedroom house with a maid to take care of all my needs, such as cleaning, cooking, laundry etc. I remember when I was working in the city where I used to live, sleeping near the bathroom using boxes as beds. Before that, I was living in the theatre and then renting an apartment with more than 10 people living in it. I am thinking and comparing my life then and now, even previously, so that I can find balance in what I do and decide.

The Lord has given me grace all along. However, in the situation I have with BreadWinnerMan, I must analyze these things to act and decide. First, I do not need to work; second, I am provided; 3) I have a maid; and 4) I have a driver driving a Mercedes Benz sports style. Such a privilege, I thought. However, I must obey whatever BreadWinnerMan has to say or command. Something to think about, I said to myself, but the big house, the maid, and my own driver and guard such a luxurious lifestyle. In addition, every week, he would give me money for whatever I needed to buy. Wow! I thought, such a good life in comparison to what I had in my previous living situation before I met him. In the beginning, I felt like I was winning the lottery. I enjoyed it in the beginning.

"Good morning, ma'am; here is your breakfast," Nori said. "Wait! Nori, I'd like to eat in the dining room, and besides, you don't have to serve me; I can do it myself." I begged. "Oh! No, ma'am, this is my job, and Sir told me to do whatever he commanded. Nori nervously explained. "Where is Mang Moises, Nori?" I wondered. "Oh! He is gardening and guarding the gate." Nori said. "Guarding the gate? For what?" I was surprised. "Ma'am, I have to go; I have to clean the house now." Nori insisted. I went downstairs and looked for Mang Moises. I found Mang Moises in his little resting place, cleaning something. I wanted to surprise

Mang Moises, so I slowly went inside his resting place and surprised him. But instead, he surprised me, knowing that I was heading to his location. "Good morning, Ma'am," Mang Moises greeted.

I was also suddenly greeted by Mang Moises. I asked Mang Moises what he was doing. He answered me, "You are not supposed to be down here in this area, ma'am." Mang Moises said in a very low voice. The belief was that it was a place for the maid and driver or guard; I was not supposed to be in that place because it was on a lower level. That's only for people who are servicing their boss. I asked Mang Moises, "Why? I could not go wherever I wanted to go." I spoke. "No, you can't, Ma'am, because this area is only for workers in this house you are living in." Mang Moises said in a little annoyed voice. Sir will get upset if we don't follow his rules.

After Mang Moises' explanation, I went back upstairs and cried. I am thinking why everybody was like a zombie. I couldn't comprehend what was going on. Until then, I fall asleep thinking why, why, why. In my situation in a big house with a maid, driver, and a guard, I felt like I was a captive, a prisoner, that was. I do not work. I can't contact my family, and I cannot do anything in the house I am living in because the maid would take over what I want to do. In addition, I can't go around the house too much because it's the place for maid, driver, and other workers' place. However, I felt comfortable due to the provision, but on the other hand, I felt like I was in prison, cornered and pressured. Although I was provided, I felt suffocated by my situation. After many years, these activities repeated, and I could not take it anymore.

After many months, it became years of living in this place of privilege. Therefore, my brain was busy thinking, and suddenly, I had an idea; I avoided Nori, my maid, and Mang Moises, my driver and guard. If I need something, they are there for me, but this time, I will try not to want anything so that I will be able to avoid them. Before I did anything, I asked my maid for a snack. "Nori, Nori, where are you? Where are you, Nori? I need some snacks. Can you come over here?" I was a little frustrated calling Nori. "Yes, Ma'am, I will be right back with your snack, ma'am. Nori said. "Wait, don't call me ma'am, call me Sofia. By the way, I don't need a snack, stay here; I must ask you some questions. We've been here for more than a year now.

Where did you come from, Nori? And where did you use to live? I asked. "Sir, pick me up at the Agency to be your maid," Nori explained. "Okay, I understand that. How about things like, I couldn't go around here, you always follow your Sir all the time, and I couldn't do that, and couldn't do this, like, you must serve me all the time. Why is that? I asked. "Mr. BreadWinnerMan told me to serve you, ma'am.

That's the only thing why he is paying me, and I need money for my family, so I must obey everything he says and commands, ma'am." Nori explained. "Again, don't call me ma'am. I understand, but there is something missing here." I was confused and insisted on knowing. "What do you mean, ma'am something is missing," Nori asked. "A puzzle—a puzzle that I couldn't solve. I don't know what it is, but there is something that is puzzling me; I will find it out myself. Don't worry; go back to what you are doing, Nori. Thank you anyway." Months and months passed by, but the puzzle was still there, and I couldn't solve it. One day, I went to the window, and I was looking for a place where I could have some adventure. Looking at the four corners of my room and metal windows, there was no way I could find an adventure to do. I must solve the hidden issues in my situation, I thought.

I silently went to the kitchen, and the door was unlocked; I went out and climbed up the back window and climbed up the fence not to open the gate. I intently wore flat shoes for easy climbing out the window with a ladder in the back. I reached down to the back of the fence facing the road, and there was a taxi passing by. I raised my hand for the taxi to stop. I then had a ride for me to go to the theatre to watch a movie. While I was at the movie, I had popcorn with some candy and soda. I enjoyed the movie and being free, with no watchful eyes around at all times. Well, there was no cell phone at that time, in the 1970s, so I had to call a taxi through the phone booth after the movie or stay at the side of the road to watch a taxi pass by. After the movie, I plan to go shopping and enjoy the city by myself without a guard or a driver.

After shopping, the taxi was waiting for me nearby, and I told him I would pay him for the time he was waiting for me while I was shopping. I am enjoying my freedom. I then use the same taxi to go home. The taxi dropped me off near the kitchen. I climbed up from the back fence in the kitchen facing the road and went through the screen door kitchen that was opened in the last five hours after I left. I changed my T-shirt and pants clothes that I wore going to the movie and did my shopping. I then wear the clothes BreadWinnerMan wants me to always wear once he is present: the see-through nighties with perfume slippers match with the nighties. I pretended I was asleep the whole five hours. I shrugged my hair a little bit to look like a mess and made the bed a little bit messy for Nori to clean up and to be fixed. I made the bathroom messy a little bit and dropped some toilet paper on the floor for Nori to clean.

Although I was provided with everything I needed, I felt like this was a pretentious type of lifestyle, and I started *not* to like it. I was naïve and asked myself why I must do these things for him. I try to analyze and use my common sense and wisdom, which I must do next. I try to realign my thoughts on what to say and how to say it. I wrote down all the questions I must ask BreadWinnerMan, the man who provided me with richness in life and privilege, which most women would love to have, but once you are in that possession, you will not like it because it feels like you are in jail or a prisoner.

I want freedom and to be able to think on my own. I am able to do things that I would like to do. Nori and my driver didn't notice my escape through the window, and everything went normal that day.

That day, he came and greeted me and said, "Hi, my dear beautiful darling, how's my beautiful flower? Did they take good care of you?" "Oh! Yes, they did take good care of me well. I got what I wanted, and everything is fine." I answered. After an hour of caressing each other, he fell asleep. I was busy looking through his pocket. I was looking for the puzzle I couldn't solve since the beginning of our relationship. However, I could not take it anymore; I woke him up. "Bread Winner Man, wake up; I need to talk to you. Why can't I go outside and make friends? I asked. "Sofia dear, whatever I said, you must follow me; this is for your own good. I gave everything for your needs, and why can't you give things for me ." He explained with sounds of annoyance. "What do you mean? I asked him and was very puzzled again by his answer. I just didn't get it.

"As I told you, I'll give you everything you need, and all you must do is follow my command. Didn't we agree with that? He angrily explained. "Fine," I said. "Now, change your clothes because they are sticky," he said. "Because of that ice cream you ate, you drop something on your clothes. I said to him, *"You are a wild animal,"* I brusquely answered. I called my maid, Nori, to clean the room and pick up the ice cream I dropped on the floor. He commanded Nori to clean up the room. "Yes, Sir." Nori obeyed without hesitation. "Nori, go back to your quarter, and I will clean this mess," I said. He disagrees with me cleaning the room. No. Nori is to clean the room; that is her job, not yours. Sit down beside me and let Nori do it. That's the reason why I hired a maid, okay?" I responded with a gush and sigh. With those feelings, sighs, and gush, he asked me, "What's the matter, darling? I'm assuming with those sighs and gush that you are not satisfied with your life with me. I have provided you with everything."

I am trying to analyze this man. I think BreadWinnerMan did not understand that I am not always looking for contentment in life and provisions. He thinks I need this and that. The luxurious lifestyle and finances he had given me were just temporary and very disturbing situations, I thought. I found out that I needed to do something. I have the feeling of doing something to be productive. Also, what I need is freedom and the ability to do things in the house. In my life with him, I feel like I am cornered, captive, and in prison. Somehow, he didn't get it. He continued asking, "Is there anything you want that I did not provide?" He asked. I do not know what to ask or what to say because it seems everything is mixed.

After many days of trying to solve the puzzles, I am thinking about what I need to do next and what to say to him. I finally found something that was totally different from what my situation was at that time. The things I need, his lifestyle, and my situation need to change. Again, I needed to talk to him, and I suggested having a business like a coffee shop or a canteen. It didn't take long, he agreed. Therefore, right away, BreadWinnerMan was looking for an area to rent to open, like a snack bar where people can come to have coffee and sandwiches to grab for breakfast and lunch. That month, we started it, and his younger brother was helping me with preparing and cooking. I hired 2 servers. It was smooth for a while until my server was sick and decided not to work for a while. I had to cover the responsibility. I made friends and connections, which was very pleasing to me as to being able to be productive. However, this canteen lasted only about a year, and I must settle down again due to my pregnancy. My EldestSon was born in the month of October in the year 1982.

Months pass by after closing the canteen; I still have so many questions about BreadWinnerMan. Many questions still linger in my mind. Once we had time together, I would ask questions, keep them in my mind, and put the pieces together. Although I was confused, I asked him a question from a confused mind of mine. I took a deep breath and asked this question: You said before you were divorced, right? Your ex-wife was living somewhere away from where you live, right? I confusedly asked. Then I continued asking: "Where are your children? You said they are all grown up, right? "That's right," he said. They are with me, and sometimes they visit their mother where she lives. He continued.

Although he was providing me financially secure, with a home, maid, and driver/guard, I still need to know about him. It was too fast for all these benefits in my life. Not that I am complaining, but I wasn't clear where I was going with this man, the BreadWinnerMan. So, I started the conversation with him to know him from the beginning to the present time. Tell me about yourself. I asked. When you were young and today. Tell me more about you, please. I begged. Then, he started telling me about his life. He was married when he was nineteen years old.

The story of his life when he was a teenager was a normal type of living situation in the country where he grew up. He worked at a manufacturing company owned by a Chinese man, the father of his wife, whose mother was a maid of a Chinese man. The Chinese man had an affair with his maid. The maid became his mistress. This affair was hidden from his family. The Chinese man was his boss. He chose to get married to the daughter of his boss. The wedding was arranged by the Chinese father.

Some people called this arrangement a shotgun wedding. She was older than him. When he was nineteen years of age, his wife was in her twenty-seven years of age. She was one of the daughters of a Chinese businessman who had many wives. She was the daughter of a Chinese man's maid or servant. Her father had an affair with his maid or servant, who is her mother. BreadWinnerMan works for this Chinese man. He and the Chinese man had an agreement to marry his maid's daughter. The Chinese man promised him half of the business would be his once he married the daughter of the Chinese man's maid.   Then BreadWinnerMan accepts the deal and marries the daughter of a Chinese man's maid or servant. Both bore five children in total. They were all grown up when I met BreadWinnerMan in the 1970s at the restaurant where I used to work. His wife is a gambler. After many years of marriage, they were trying to get a divorce, but there was no divorce in that country. If pursued, the couple must wait 7 years to be approved to get a divorce, or it might not be approved. The BreadWinnerMan got a piece of his father-in-law's business, and he worked hard to make this business bigger than his father-in-law's.

One day, BreadWinnerMan wants me to see his manufacturing with 100 employees. "Come on, come with me." Where? I asked. "I'll show you the factory." Oh! Really, okay! I said and dressed up and hopped in the Sporty Mercedes Benz with him. It was so quiet the first time, and music was on to listen to. After a hundred miles away, he slowed down. "What's wrong? I asked. I must leave you here. He explained with worries in his eyes. I was puzzled, and I asked why. He continued saying, "I have to leave you here in this little store." But I don't know these people. I said in a worrisome voice; my eyes and tears started to come out. I said with worry and very puzzled in my mind. Well, I will introduce you and me to these people in this store.

Then you could stay and talk to them while I am going to the factory. I thought you were going to show me your factory. But I can't right now. He answered with worry in his face. I was puzzled by him on why he must leave me in that store. Please, please just obey me, okay? To my confusion, I agreed because my mind was trying to solve the puzzle, and I said it was okay for him to leave me in that store. He continued driving by himself towards the factory. I was unable to see the factory inside the store, but up the hill, I was able to look at the surroundings, but not too clearly due to trees blocking my vision.

It was a very nice area. It seemed like rich people lived up there. I asked the saleslady of the store. "Oh yes! That factory up there they have around a hundred workers. They always have visitors. I could see cars passing by and parked up the hill. Who are those people you know? I asked out of curiosity. It seemed like they had businesspeople coming up there, and sometimes they had parties like a celebration. "Uhmm!" The store lady said. She also sounds curious. I was curious too.

After an hour of waiting, BreadWinnerMan came back to pick me up from the little store he had left me. "Come on, come on, hurry!" He commanded. I was confused as to why he was so anxious to leave. Why? Why must I hurry to come into the car?" I curiously asked. "Just hurry! Okay!" He brusquely commended. I waved to the saleslady of the store, and he took off and drove as fast as he could. "What is wrong with you? I asked confusedly. It seemed like someone was chasing you! What is going on? I pressed the questions. I want to know this man who I have been living with for 2 days a week for more than two years at that time. "I am sorry to do this to you," He apologized. "What do you mean?" I was confused, and I cried of confusion maybe, or for my life that was questionable, or the path of my life was not clear, but it seemed like it was hard to give up the good living provided by this man financially, home, maid, driver, and guard.

One day, I must research more about BreadWinnerMan's life. I thought. I cannot just ignore this issue being with this man with a secret life who seems very anxious, worried, and stressed out of something I do not understand and don't know what it was. I questioned myself as to whether I could just take advantage of a good living. However, remember my last experience sleeping in the box bed near the bathroom or in the theatre. I forced myself to stay with him due to the benefits and good life regarding finance, maid, driver, guard, and, of course, the Mercedes. I feel like I am important and special. But what pulls me back is the hidden questions with blurred answers. I am living an abundant lifestyle, but there is something within that is not clear and needs a solution, or else I will not have peace. Peace is my best friend. I asked myself what do I want in my life? What else do I want in my life? In comparison to having all abundance with a maid and a guard to serve me.

Furthermore, it was Thursday; I forgot that this was the day BreadWinnerMan came by to see me in my 4 bedroom house with maids and a driver that he provided. Again, I tried to get away from him for a while by not greeting him coming out the door. Instead, I climbed up the window again and ran away, calling a taxi for a ride to my favorite theatre. He was looking for me, and he could not find me in the house. He was panicking and worried. He called the maid and the driver and asked questions such as questions of an anxious and angry man. Nori said that she was in the bathroom, and Mang Moises had no answer at all.

The chaos just started. I felt like I was missing a purpose or seeking my own creativity. I need a clear mind of who I am living with this man, and what's going on in my life suddenly became abundant. Not that I like being poor and having nothing at all, but the puzzle of this man is killing me. While I was at the movie theatre, I was enjoying my privilege as a free woman. I had popcorn and M&M snacks. Yes. Finally. I am free. Free temporarily, but I treasure that moment of being ME. Being me with nobody watching and driving me to wherever I wanted to go. After the movie, the taxi was waiting for me outside the theatre, and I went home like there was nothing wrong, pretending I had a normal lifestyle. It takes about an hour from the city to where I live.

Meanwhile, BreadWinnerMan came to the house, and I was not there to be found, it may seem. "Mang Moises! Where is she?"

he asked angrily. "Nori, Nori, where is your ma'am? "Sir, I don't know. I was in the bathroom cleaning." Nori cried. "I hired you to watch her, didn't I? This is your job to watch her, isn't it?" he angrily said. "Yes, Sir," Nori answered. "Mang Moises, come with me. Nori, watch the phone." He commanded. They went downtown to look for me. Meanwhile, I was approaching the house in the backyard. I went through the fence and got inside my bedroom while they were going out in the Mercedes to find me in the city. I immediately changed my clothes, checked the calendar and time, and reminded myself about the time and days he came to visit me. I shrugged my hair, scattered all the dirty clothes in the bathroom, and hid the clothes I was wearing to the movie.

I pretended I had just woken up and went to the bathroom and brushed my teeth. Suddenly, someone knocked on the door. "Yes, Nori, I just woke up, then I pretended I was yawning. You could give me my snack later, okay? I'd like to go back to bed. I'll call you later." I said to my maid and pretended I was yawning again. "Ma'am, ma'am, I need to talk to you," Nori said shakenly and begged. I answered, Get away!" I am still sleepy. "But ma'am, Sir was here to see you." I opened the door hurriedly and asked, "What?" What did he say? Tell me, tell me. I nervously asked my maid. "They went to downtown to look for you," Nori said. "Oh my God! I was scared.

"Where were you ma'am? Nori asked. "Nori, I went out and

watched a movie. Don't tell your sir okay? I can't stand here in my bedroom all day. I will die. I cried. I need to go somewhere, I got bored. Suddenly, someone approached the door, slammed the door and yelled. "Nori, Nori!" BreadWinnerMan angrily called Nori. Nori came out and didn't say anything about me. After a while, "Sir, Ma'am is in her bedroom waiting for you." Nori calmly said. "Yes Sir...?" We didn't see her when I came this morning! Where the hell was, she! He questioned with an angry annoyed voice.

I came out from the bedroom yawning and scattered my hair stretching my arms and covered my mouth yawning, and said, "Hi darling! I am still sleepy come up hurry" I said it and romantically sounded. "Where were you.? We were looking for you. Don't lie to me." "We need to talk." BreadWinnerMan rushing upstairs. "Okay! I'll tell you the truth. I spoke. I was trying to cover up my escape plan coiling my finger to BreadWinnerMan's shirts to unbutton, and said to me "I do not want you to go out without my permission, is that clear?" "How could I get your permission if I can't call you?" I spoke. "You must wait until I come here or asked me in advance "Okay! I kissed him to remove the upset face and behavior. It worked.

Hunting of me downtown is over. Months, and months passed, I always stayed in my room. I could see the steel window and four corners of my bedroom. The sun was shining given the brightness of its rays, and the moon at night gives shady light away from the darkness. The howl of wolf I could hear, the cry of crickets I can't bear. Come, come morning please give another light to shine the darkest side. Wait, wait, still thinking whether to get out of these situations, whether to leave all these ambitions. Ambitions to stay away from meager life. Is it survival to live up then what? Is it that when we give up something, then we lose everything? Do we really lose everything? Those are the questions in my mind that I must analyze and study myself on what truly the meaning of happiness and freedom is.

However, after seeing a doctor, I found out that I am pregnant. Now, I do really need Nori, my maid and my driver. I continued my lifestyle with abundance but there was sometimes a feeling of being captive. I am still not settled within my mind that I can't do what I wanted to do. It seems like paralyzing me in that regard. I must do something to feel free and being capable using my capabilities within. After how many months carrying my precious baby boy, BreadWinnerMan and I talk again about what needs to be done for me to be useful I would say. So, he planned a business for me to do and managed. I was very excited.

One day, I decided to make a decision that might not be right, but I believe it gives me the freedom I want. I talked to him about my situation. I told him that this is not the life I want. I do not need to have a maid, driver, and guard in my life. I do not need a big house and all the money you have given me every week. I do not need those. What I need is *freedom.* That's it. He was very surprised at my longing and wants in life, freedom. He told me that if I want, we can open a business in America.

Meaning, he wants me to come to America. Then, my thought rush in two ways No or Yes because I do not know America. I've heard that America does not have servants to help, and I must do all household works such as house cleaning, cooking, and other household responsibilities. If you want to have servants, you must be rich and able to afford to pay for their service. At the same time, I feel like I am free if I am in America. As my father says when I was young "America is heaven." So, I am so confused at that moment of my life on what I need to do.

BreadWinnerMan asked me again if I wanted to go to America, and he would process the paperwork as soon as possible. I told him to give me time to think about it. I do not know anyone in America, and it seems that's a faraway place; it seems like somewhere. I can remember when I was young, at 10 years of age. My father was telling me about America after I told him about my dream. I was dreaming about a huge airplane with colors red and gray up in the sky, and I was a giant child in my dream. My father interprets my dream and says to me that I will be going to many places, and this is America. My father said, "America is heaven," and people are free as they are practicing *freedom.* Again, I am puzzled. I question myself: what is *freedom?* When I was 24 years of age, America was still a puzzling place to me.

I asked BreadWinnerMan with a puzzled voice, "is America somewhere over the rainbow, like what my had father said, "America is heaven." I asked him a little puzzling question. He explained where America is, and he knows people in the Embassy. He will be able to process papers as soon as possible if I want to go to America. Because of my curiosity about America, I agreed. Also, there were times I was afraid to go to America. It seems like it's another world to me, an unfamiliar world, that is.

However, I agreed with his plan on what we are going to do in the USA, and here I have been in the USA since year 1984. I've been here in America for more than 39 years since writing this Memoir. I could not forget my luxurious lifestyle and forgetting to be thankful of everything I got due to my conscience I had of just being a mistress, living with a man part time, with everything I need in my life were provided by the BreadWinnerMan. Reminiscing was the only thing I could do and move on in life forward, not backward.

CHAPTER TEN

Looking Back My Luxurious Lifestyle: The World Expo "84"

After my agreement with BreadWinnerMan to come to America, the process of documentations and passport was quickly processed. Looking back on my previous luxurious lifestyle, my faith has been tested again. I came to America hired by Chinese company, Lucky Company in April 1984 landed in New York with 29 more workers hired by the company. Then we moved to New Orleans. The company's bus took us to New Orleans where the World Expo 84 will be held. There were more than 30 people hired by Lucky Company coming from the Philippines and China. All of us were on the company's bus heading to New Orleans for World Expo 84 event.

In the beginning, it was a very strange feeling to work with a company; I was one of the workers. My life changed in a different direction, and I could not accept it as a worker due to the fact that I had servants, and a driver in my own country. I was assigned to wash dishes in the restaurant part of the World Expo 84, managed by the husband of the daughter of my son's godmother. A huge kitchen and a huge washing spray bigger than I am. I was perfectly devastated. I fought back. My pride was tested. It was totally the opposite position I had when I was in my home country. My position as a boss and a princess in my own country differs from that of what I experienced in the USA, the land of the free, they called it. To analyze as a privilege in my own country, I had maids, a driver, and a guard, and now living in America, I am washing dishes, which I was not able to wash dishes in my home country because I had maids or shall I say "servants" taking care of all household responsibilities. Also, I thought America was heaven, as my father says when I was young at 10 years of age.

After many complaints and hesitations being assigned to the kitchen to wash dishes, I finally was assigned to one of the many departments at World's Fair Expo 1984, where inlaid mother-of-pearl furniture and handmade carpets made by the Chinese people. Once I was assigned to this department, I sold many items in bulk. As a salesperson at "World Expo in New Orleans," my pursuit and determination to move forward in the beginning assigned as a dishwasher, I became a salesperson with the highest sold items in the department of furniture and appliances inlaid with mother of pearl, the very expensive items in the department of the "World's Fair 1984 Expo" event.

Coming to America hired by Chinese company to work at World Expo, I unknowingly was assigned in the restaurant washing dishes. I totally refused. I complained. However, in that department no one listens to me instead management laughs at me and disregards my complaints. I walked through the gift shop with wet boots full of water and the gift shop floor water draining to every corner of the store. Some of giftshop workers were puzzled by what I am doing and called a janitor to dry the floor to avoid customer accidents. My co-workers and customers were watching and talking to each other while I was walking like a fashion model of wet full of water boots wearing dirty wet apron. I walked and walked all the way to the manager's office, Lina, which was on the other side of the huge building of the World Expo. I decided to knock on the door of the general manager's office to request a reassignment of job responsibility in any department but not in the kitchen washing dishes.

I kept knocking on her office door, but she didn't open the door. I tried again and again, and I knocked on the door so loudly to make sure the sound of my knocks would hurt her two ears. Through my persistent behavior to talk to her and begged with voice tone of an angry woman to be removed from washing dishes responsibility in the kitchen, the manager finally assigned me in the gift shop. First, I was tested to see if I have a good customer service approach to gift shop visitors. There were many trials and observations from the general manager. I somehow managed it to the point that all my action was just pretention as giving a good customer service to pass the many trials. I've been through many trials with eyes everywhere watching me how to approach a customer.

At least Gift Shop was much better than washing dishes I thought. I remembered those huge utensils in the kitchen as a small stature woman, I was having difficulty lifting those machines, and I am not used to wash dishes since that I used to have maids, guard, and driver in my own country. Since I was assigned to the gift shop, I must be good at it. I must pass the observation and trials here, I thought. The many observations and trials, I must act and serve the visiting customers in the gift shops in a courteous, respectful, good manner greeting, and the best customer service ever. Every customer I would say "Good Morning Ma'am, how can I help you ma'am?" with a big smile.

This courteous manner I have developed, benefiting me and the department I served. I sold many items in the gift shops, and I was transferred to another department with the highest cost items to be sold. I used my "good manners and right conduct" with a smile greeting customers and again I sold many items. Proving this type of technique, I would use the same tactics in case I am assigned to another department. I learned that customers were unable to refuse my sales pitch.

I remember my technique selling items past at the gift shop. Innocently approaching them with smiles, and respect in a courteous manner, I sold many items. The gift shop had the highest sold items and the highest sales income that week I was assigned. My general manager was very happy with my performance. However, some of my co-workers were jealous of my performance and they would tease me and would call me the" favorite sales lady" with smirk smiles at me. My co-workers developed a doubtful mind and were very jealous of me as the manager always favored me. My life then became miserable due to jealousy of my co-workers. Six of my co-workers (the bad girl's group) planned on how to bring me down.

One day, my two co-workers who knew the plan of these six girls to punch and to bring me down to the ground separated silently from these six bad girls and talked to me secretly. These 2 friends of mine were like my secret agent telling me what the Bad Girls Group was planning for me to bring me down to the ground. The next morning, the company driver was picking up all the workers. We were on the bus from our apartment we were staying heading to the World's Expo stores.

Therefore, my 2 best friends protected me while I was inside the bus. We were on the bus heading to work. This bus is from Lucky Company, it's a private bus for this company. That early morning inside the bus I was so puzzled why my friend Percy said to me to sit down near by her, Perla, and the driver. I did. After realigning ourselves (3 of us) in the front seat here comes the 6 mean girls who planned to bring me down to the ground because they thought I was the spy girl. They pulled my long black hair and punched me and grabbed me trying to push me around. I was puzzled on what was going on and cried. My friends Percy and Perla protected me from these six mean girls. The driver commanded these 6 mean girls to go back to the back of the bus as soon as possible. The driver counted- one, two, three…..and he stood up away from the stirring wheel and pushed one of the bad girls. Therefore, six of them ran towards the back of the bus.

I asked Percy and Perla why they were so upset with me and why they were trying to hurt me. I do not understand at all. Percy told me she would explain it to me later where no one can listen and see us talking about the Six Bad Girls Group. After we were dropped off at the stores in the World 84 Expo building, Percy told me to come to her department and we will talk, and she answered my very strange question. I did ask many questions in our break time, and the story begins.

These Six Mean Bad Girls were suspected that I was the spy for Lina, the general manager because they were stealing merchandise in the gift shop store. Every time the department closes at closing time, one of these 6 girls would pack some merchandise and bring it to her car or someone's car. Each one would get their turn to steal merchandise. Each one would do the same every night at closing time. One day, Percy told me that night 3 of them would steal merchandise and someone would bring it to somewhere where they would send this stolen merchandise to their country and sell it there.

After knowing what they were doing, I went to the phone booth at 9 pm and called the general manager, Lina. I said, "Lina, you must call the police to catch these girls stealing merchandise at the gift shop." I told Lina to call the police now, as soon as possible. Lina asked me who I was, and I told her there was no need to know my name. I hung up the booth phone. Until recently, no one knew who called Lina to tell her to call the police to capture these 6 girls stealing merchandise at the gift shop. Even my friends Percy and Perla didn't know who told Lina about this activity of the six bad girls. Most of these girls were deported to their country, and two escaped without their passports. All passports of these girls were confiscated by the police that came to that department at the time they were stealing merchandise. Some of them were arrested at that time, and the rest were caught in their boarding house, packing to run away.

Although I went through these many odd events in my life, there was always a reason why this happened. Amazing! I do believe that whatever happened, it was meant to be. Again, writing this memoir of mine, I now have the full answers to each tragic incident I went through with these six bad girls. Then, I could see why it happened, and my questions and puzzled thoughts were solved and answered. I have been asking the Lord, why, why me? I am thankful to the Lord that He is always with me and being with me, protecting me from every disastrous event that comes to my life while temporarily walking through my journey here on earth of plenty.

However, after a six-month contract, the company rehired me to work for them in New York. I was thinking, "Shall I work and accept this assignment to be assigned in New York? The company will be the one to renew my passport for an extension of 6 months. Working in New York was another different story. I remember when I was at the World Expo, the Chinese do not speak the English language. They usually speak their own language. I have a problem with that because I do not know what they are talking about; it is as if they were talking about me, and I do not understand. Two things in my mind at that time: I needed a job, and Lucky Company would extend my worker's visa, so I accepted it. In October 1984, I worked with Lucky Company in New York City, New York.

After working with this company for a year in 1984, I decided to move forward and went to Houston, Texas, where I accepted a job with a higher income than in New York hired by the Chinese company. I have always taken advantage of many opportunities. From then on, that was my way, and I always learned from the experience, using these experiences to develop new skills. In learning from these experiences and challenges, I considered these as my accumulated "life tools." These many experiences have given me the opportunity to move forward in a positive manner, benefit from it, and become knowledgeable of life's struggles and how to survive many challenges in this world of plenty. I survived and protected from these 6 mean girls, and I learned tools and skills on how to avoid or protect myself from these types of people.

When it comes to knowledge and learning, an opportunity comes to my doorstep to attend training, meetings, and classes. I always take advantage and make the time to participate. Currently, while writing this book, The River of Life: The Memoir, I am a published author, visual artist, and entrepreneur doing business as a Notary Public and art Teacher. I was a landlord previously before my rental properties sold and got hit with Covid   19   and   the Sallie Hurricane in September 2020.

Now, after a disastrous life came to our lives with my previous husband Thomas, the COVID, sickness, flood, and death, I still survived, but I went through lots of disastrous life experiences. These experiences, such as flooding, have given me other tools and skills, strengthening and skillful in life while continuing my journey here on earth of plenty. Sally's Hurricane in September 2020 again became my tools to survive in any disastrous comes to life. I titled it "The River of Life: The Memoir." It was such a memorable moment, and although I called it a "disastrous" experience, these experiences have given me the strengths and skills to survive whatever disastrous comes to life while living here on earth moving forward.

After being a widow, I was living by myself after my

previous husband, Thomas, passed away in December 2020. It was a very lonely place to be by myself. Although I met lots of men, my interest in dating was not in my mind at the time of grieving my previous husband's passing. I grieved and cried by myself in my newly renovated cabana where I was living, which was secluded in almost 3 acres of land with a gate.

Anyway, I met a man in July 2022, a responsible, peaceful, and respectful man, and I got married in November 2022. With a new man in my life, I enjoy the traveling we do together. We have plans and goals to continue our activities. He plays guitar, and does woodworking art. I will continue my book writing, and painting artwork on canvas.

Sometimes, we paint on canvas and we sing karaoke together. I have such as wonderful time with the man I married in November 2022. Living such as wonderful life and finding a man with whom I am able to freely express our indifferences while living in the world of plenty and privilege, I am grateful and thankful to the Lord.

My life has settled down, but since then, I have been writing my book titled "The Memoir: The River of Life." in my mind, there it lingers the memories from a long time ago. I remember those years when my first husband, now ex-husband, left us for another woman while I was working more than 10 hours a day. Again, all the struggles and trials passed, and I became stronger than ever before. I may sound and look like a fragile woman from the outside, but from the inside, I am well-rehearsed due to many disastrous experiences I've been through in my life, such as the experience I had at the World Expo 84 with these 6 mean girls.

I am so thankful to my friends Percy, Perla, and the driver for protecting me from these mean girls, and of course, the Lord was and is with me every day; therefore, I formed a group called Sofia's Prayer is Powerful group which I have more than 300 members that included the group with more members who participated with my group. Thank you, Lord. As my tools to be strong continue, *"The Trashing Floors"* is my next chapter, which is about when I got divorced in the year 1997 from my now ex-husband, whom we call in the next chapter *Ex-Husband*, and then the story begins.

CHAPTER ELEVEN

The Trashing Floors

From Germany in year 1986 to 1989 then moved to Hawaii from 1989 to 1991, the story begins. I petitioned my mother to come to Hawaii to live with us. My mother accompanied my EldestSon at eight years of age to come to America to join with us in year 1991. I found a job in Hawaii to work in the banking industry in 1989. Due to my Ex-Husband's assignment in military to New Jersey, we moved from Hawaii to New Jersey in year 1992. We settled down in the Bayville area while I was working at the title division as a title agent with K. Hovnanian company, one of the ten largest real estate developer companies in New Jersey, and all-over United State of America. It was costly to live in New Jersey therefore, I was looking for another job at Federal Credit Union assigned as an EDP processor encoding checks or any paper money and calculate all work from the teller line. My duty hours was to begin after the bank is closed, at 5 pm. My Ex-Husband at the time as a husband was assigned at Fort Monmouth Military Base in Eatontown, New Jersey.

After how many months of being in New Jersey, my Ex-Husband was assigned back to Germany for more than two years and we got divorced in 1997 and my life has changed completely because he forgot or intently forgot to support 2 boys aged 8 and 13.

My children and I went to unimaginable distraction of life, hunger, cold in the winter without heater, and foreclosure of 4 bedrooms home with an in-ground swimming pool. These days, that is how easy it is to ruin a striving family with children. I asked for help at the welfare center, and I was not approved due to my accumulated investments such as five lots that I bought in Ocala Florida in year 1985 and a residence with 4 bedrooms and in-ground swimming pool in New Jersey.

Because of pride, I could not face myself filling in line to ask for food stamps. I could not, and I did not. I went home and hid myself in my bedroom and cried for hours only to realize that I had two children to be fed. I must do something. Instead, I quit my job to have time for my children from K.Hovnanian real estate developer in New Jersey as a title agent, and I withdrew my 401K and savings to pay bills.

From 1985 to 1997 there were many traveling assignments to military bases in many different states and countries. I quit traveling with him due to my work duties and children to take care of and to permanently be in the school for their education purposes. Our marriage collapsed due to many responsibilities and job assignments, and I was busy with my work such as at the time I was working with a Title Company, and part time at Credit Union. When Ex-Husband found another woman in his life from the bar, I also removed his name and closed the checking account we used to share for household expenses, and house mortgage.

When the money runs out, I have nowhere to get cash, but my first survival instinct was to seek food in the pantry that was forgotten, the noodles and cans of soups. Also, I go to Food Mart and look for sale food like bread inside the cart. These breads are to be thrown out by Food Mart but I know the days that they would throw the leftover food so I would go to Food Mart and buy those bread for only 50 cent or 20 cent a bag. My children ate noodles and leftover food for almost a year before I was able to sort things out on what to do next.

In the beginning, well to protect his reputation let us call him my "Ex-Husband" who was a soldier in year 1985. I met him in New Orleans at World Expo 84, then I also met again in Houston Texas in 1985. After my contract with the Chinese company, I switched job and the people I know from New Orleans had given me the opportunity to work for them. They have businesses such as perfume stores, restaurants, and providing food, and products in the ship parked at the shipyard of Houston Texas and Galveston. Then, I met him again in the restaurant where all the soldiers ate and gathered in that area.

While going to the store in that restaurant, I also help the restaurant if they need my help besides being in the Perfume Store. I had multiple responsibilities, and meeting lots of people. I met my

Ex-Husband again and we went through remembering the past while he was visiting the World Expo at that time in the years 1984 to 1985. This reminiscing put us back to becoming friends again. Then we started dating. Perhaps, after 3 to 4 months he proposed. We then arranged the date of marriage.

However, my Ex-Husband must go back to Germany for his assignment. I then followed him after my graduation from Houston Texas School of Business, taking Office Automation Program that year of 1985-1986. In the airport heading to the place in Ansbach where Ex-Husband was assigned, I was held in the airport guarded with lots of police around me. I do not know what the hold was about, but Ex-Husband came to the airport, and I was released. The reason for the hold was that my papers or passport were not updated. All paper works and issues about me being in Germany was solved. I then went with Ex-Husband riding in a military jeep heading to his apartment in Ansbach Germany. It feels like we just know each other at that moment.

However, I felt like we were new and didn't know each other. I was bored and after a week of being in Ansbach Germany, I was looking for something to do. I then volunteered at Army Community Service after a month of being with my Ex-Husband. I took care of soldiers who were assigned to Ansbach Germany. I processed their dental and medical records. When assigned, I also brief them at the Briefing Room and explain to them their assignment location, and what to expect in that location. I also toured their families in the surrounding areas, giving the families their needs such as plates, cookers, beds, blankets, etc. until they get their shipped household from USA to Germany.

The first thing I've been with Ex-Husband when I joined with him, he was somehow detached and the feeling of isolation. That was my first impression of him when I first joined with him in Germany. I believe at that time it was just a little feeling of isolation because we didn't really have time for each other when he visited the USA because of other responsibilities we have encountered. By the way, he was only 19 years old, and I was 27 years old when we got married in year 1985.

The same month I got hired to dispatch soldiers and prepare their documents such as medical and dental documents. I met friends and I also continued my Avon products to sell in Germany like what I was doing in Houston Texas part time. I got pregnant and we had a little boy in year 1987. We named him in this book DoctorSon. Ex-Husband, the father of DoctorSon was a quiet man. He doesn't talk a lot. I am the talker. I would always release what I have in my mind. You will know who I am based on what comes out from my mouth coming from my brain. You will know the type of personality I am.

Anyway, after five years in Germany, my Ex-Husband was

assigned to Schofield Barracks in Hawaii. At that time my youngest son and I must travel with my husband, now Ex-husband. My son, whom now we call DoctorSon was only nine months old. After settling in Hawaii in Honolulu, I found a job at First Hawaiian Bank. Taking classes in Banking at the community college in Honolulu, I was accepted as an EDP processor. I processed checks encoding in balancing paper money at the main office of First Hawaiian Bank in downtown Honolulu; after many months of working at First Hawaiian bank in the downtown main branch, I moved to a branch in Wahiawa, where we lived nearby. I settled in Wahiawa First Hawaiian Bank to be a Customer Service Representative. I was the one who took care of customers who had complaints and issues with their accounts and gave them help in processing their applications, etc. I then used my knowledge from taking Certification classes for Customer Service and using my knowledge while I was at the World Expo 84 in New Orleans.

After his assignment in Hawaii, we moved to New Jersey in the year 1992. I was looking for a job, and I found a job at K. Hovnanian, the largest real estate developer in New Jersey. I worked at the Title Division as a title agent. First, I must go to school to be certified at Rutger's University and to be licensed as a Title Agent. After passing the test, I became a Title Agent, and my next responsibility was to process search surveys from 20 to 60 years of ownership and type documentation process to be recorded in the county of the land origin location. I also train new onboard employees in that department of the Title Division from K. Hovnanian. I may not be able to fit in here all the experiences I have had while living in New Jersey with my now Ex-Husband since 1997 for more than 11 years, from 1986 to 1997, and the 2 boys, who are now grown up and have their own children.

However, on April 27, 2023, while revising and polishing this manuscript, I found my diaries. The writings of things that happened to me and my 2 children, besides the happiness in our lives, the downside of it was hidden. However, it was written in the form of "My Diary," kind of remembering the past, not to be repeated along the way. Moving forward in life to take the positive route of my journey here on earth of plenty and to be free. Journaling and or writing experiences through forming a diary helps me to heal the wounds of the wounded and the scars while going through the downside of life. Somehow, the river of life experiences while passing through many rugged terrain. It was a long journey while still living in this world of plenty, the world of privilege and the loss I somehow still survived.

Previously, my life with my husband, now Ex-Husband since 1997, and while temporarily traveling here on earth of plenty we somehow created a terrain to follow. My adventure in life then got started.

In year 1994 my Ex-Husband and I decided to buy a beautiful property located in Bayville, New Jersey. This property had an inground swimming pool, and many trees surrounding the area. It was nearby a bay that most people would like to enjoy with. To be able to afford all necessities, I must work, and I ended up working 2 jobs in New Jersey. Ex-Husband was also working and traveling. When he comes home from traveling, he is enjoying the property we bought. Due to many travels he had to do for the military assignments, being away from family it could be that relationship may collapse. Working two jobs' exhausts me every day and sometimes enjoying the beautiful property may have diminished due to busyness of working. I sometimes come home at 11 o'clock at night. I was very exhausted when I came home late at night and I had no time for my children, which early in the morning at 5 am again, getting ready to go to work. What a life at that time. It was an exhausting lifestyle and forgot the other side of life's beauty we always had. I now learned that money is not everything you need in life.

Furthermore, Ex-Husband was traveling again, and went back to Germany, then to Korea. While I was focused on working with the Title Division at K.Hovnanian Company. Somehow, when Ex-Husband came back home to New Jersey, he was somehow detached. It was a very strange situation because he would introduce me to his friend, and this friend of his was the one who gave us a ride from the airport where Ex-Husband had to be dropped off heading to his assignment in Germany. This friend of his would stay with us and he would start cleaning our swimming pool like he lives there. Well, a week before this happened, he called and said that he needed a place to sleep, and he somehow approved by Ex-Husband, and he stayed with us, and he drove Ex-Husband to the airport with us.

This type of strange action my common sense always giving me the answer to my spiritual question. I am putting the pieces together and making sense of my Ex-Husband's action. I am always trying to solve the puzzles and analyze it and fill in with characters in my analysis in finding the solution to a very strange type of mentality. After using my common sense and analyzing it, I found out that my Ex-Husband had an affair using his friend throughout the process. Strange as may sound, the Lord is always giving me the answers to life puzzles I am in. This was how it got started in resolving the spiritual issues between me and my used-to-be husband, Ex-Husband. However, before that happened to confront the issues of the analysis result relying on my common sense, his friend had confessed to me on what had happened. Ex-Husband had a relationship with a woman he met at the bar that is.

In a relationship, there should be no hidden agenda, no secrets and it's all out to communicate and to understand who I am and what's inside my mind. I believe that being communicative to a partner would benefit both. Ex-Husband was a very silent and secretive man. I just now wondered, there could be some toxic elements that ruined his thinking because he likes to keep secrets. When we got divorced in 1997, MyDoctorSon was only 8 years old, and MyEldestSon, joined us in 1991. MyEldestSon was only 13 years old. Visiting 6 Loon Place, New Jersey, our previous home, was a spiritual battle.

My children whom I had to face and accept the reality of life journey. Remembering the happy and sad moments in this house of 4 bedrooms with underground swimming pool was hurtful and feeling broken truly such a memory will never be forgotten until these days at the present times writing "The Memoir: The River of Life" book opens the memory of my life here on earth. It meant to be that this will happen because "nothing just happened" type of event. There must be a purpose. Although, I have accepted this life journey of mine, I can't help to re-write and re-read to visualize what had just happened. I do believe that the Lord allows us to be broken and goes to struggle to come to the narrow gate and journeys in the new life beginning, the life prepared for me.

When we came inside this house, the house Ex-Husband and I bought in year 1994 which was abandoned for many months. There were bad and good memories in this four-bedroom house with an inground swimming pool. For me to accept these memories it must be reopened and re-thought the past not to repeat the pattern of life journey. Instead to rehearse and to pinpoint what had happened so pattern will not repeat. My DoctorSon was kicking and throwing some stuff along the way while getting inside the house and I could see his eyes with tears. DoctorSon was only 7 or 8 years old at that time. "Hey kiddo" I said. "I know you are hurt due to your dad, and I got divorced. However, this is the past we must endure when parents disunited. I asked DoctorSon about what's going on in his mind and what he is getting out from this abandoned house of ours? I insisted for him to get what he must pick it up from that house and let it go all the memories and pain we have encountered in this house. I told him that there will be a good life coming our way, and I am so sure of that.

What we have experience in that after and before abandonment by Ex-Husband who was attracted to another woman in the bar, my children went through reprocess of a new life. However, joy comes from struggles we endured which are always in my mind. At the time of abandonment, we didn't have heat in the winter at Loon Place New Jersey. We suffered from hunger and no electricity for six months to a year. Although we experienced cold in the winter and heat in the summertime, we were happy despite what's going on in our lives. While I was dating Thomas, my previous husband who passed away in December 2020, he would come to Loon Place to fix the issues of my house, that Ex-Husband abandoned. He would fix the pipe not to be frozen in the wintertime.

While going inside the house, I heard my son complaining about what's going on in our lives. He said, "Mommy--I hate this house. It's too quiet, and so lonely. Before--this was very happy, full of people every weekend, now--it's ugly." "What do you mean.? I asked. Yes. I know how my son felt. I felt the same. The coldness and the loneliness feeling of the house that used to be a happy family but became sad and very lonely.

Through mesmerizing the past between me and Ex-Husband, I would remember those moments when he was trying to discipline MyDoctorSon and MyEldestSon. He would use a broom and belt to punish disobedience of our children. One day, my EldestSon was punished because he broke the glass table. I would grab this belt away from him by climbing on his back. My ExHusband is much taller and much stronger than me. I would jump higher to reach the belt that he was about to hit my EldestSon, and throw the belt away far enough away from him. I fell on the floor and got hurt but I ignored the pain of my broken arm. I grabbed my EldestSon away from him and ordered him to go outside.

Every time I saw him doing these types of punishments, I would stop him by climbing on his back and grab that broom or belt he was about to hit our children. These types of behavior he had I was very alarmed. Through talking to his relatives in Hawaii such as his grandpa, I found out how he grew up with his grandpa while he was young. While we were in Germany, I spoke to his grandparents in Hawaii, and I found out that his grandparents and parents were not talking for years. The grandfather would tie him up, hang him up by his hands to punish him for disobedience when he was a boy. At the time of my call to his grandfather, his grandfather asked to talk to his grandson to ask forgiveness. However, Ex-Husband refused to talk to his grandfather on the phone. Confronting and facing the previous issues of life can heal someone who was involved at that time.

When previous issues in life are not confronted, therefore, pattern may repeat. This action now that he is a grown-up man mirroring the past through doing the same with our children. These reminiscing have given me the attitude of feeling *"it's okay for me and him to get divorce"* it meant to be. I hope that his new wife will be able to understand what, and how Ex-Husband went through while he was a boy. I also pray for both his new wife and Ex-Husband to go on in life and understand every moment of their actions and treatment of each other while living here on earth of plenty. There are always solutions from the past issues not to repeat to move forward in life. Always forgive and have peace within yourself to continue life in a positive manner.

Furthermore, telling the story of how we felt while getting inside this abandoned house of ours we used to live in; it seems very cold and dark. When you go inside this house, Loon Place, we feel coldness and loneliness. The gray and mauve color combination on the siding and window, bow windows, used to be very bright. After almost three years, it faded away. Dusty, soiled, tall grass back and front yard, abandoned lawn chairs scattered all over the backyard.

Empty swimming pool, it used to be full of water and full of happiness, now it's empty and lonely. The liner is rip and the automatic cover does not work anymore. The flower planted was still alive but thirsty and hungry for care. Things around us are just like humans. Human beings need caring also. Things like toys, pets, and almost everything also needs caring for. If abandoned, then it gets molded and looks so sad due to dust covering all toys and all abandoned things in the house because no one is using it.

My EldestSon was only 13 years old at that time, and my younger son was only eight years old. Today he is now a physician let us call him, DoctorSon. My young children at that time suggested to continue investigating the house we neglected for many months after the disunite of marriage between Ex-Husband and I. "I want to look at my bedroom upstairs, mom" said my dear DoctorSon with no smile on his face. Head, eyes, face down touching his old toys scattered around. Lifted some of his clothes, ran to the closets and stared at untouched hanging clothes. Touching smelling and stretching to see if would fit and maybe it still be the same. He dropped the clothes he was stretching and realized it would not be the same. Exactly, the same as we move along further, it will not be the same. New life begins. I was watching him how he approaches those moments, and I explained to him that life here on earth is just like plants, grow, and regrow, prune and multiply, and fertilize, then move on.

DoctorSon opened the other closet that has a hole going the other side of the attic and looked through and stared at it. Remembering where he used to hide when I came home from work. He would say, *"Look for me mommy. Find me."* DoctorSon used to say. I responded, *"If I find you, ready for a big tickle?"* My DoctorSon would say, *"Okay, but not too much." "Okay dookie, here I come."* I found him hiding in his closet where all his favorite clothes were hung with plastic hangers. *"Got you!"* I said to my son. He didn't notice that I was following his voice and I found him in the closet where he used to hide.

But suddenly, at that moment his face looked so sad, and I asked him, *"what's the matter kiddo? "I do remember mommy, I used to hide in this closet playing hide and seek with my brother."* He explained. *"I know"* I responded with a sad face. I ended that conversation right away because I felt like I did not want to go through sadness at that moment. I am focusing on what needs to be done about the abandoned 4-bedroomed house with swimming pool. *"Come on--let's go honey."* I felt like I did not want to remember all these that happened in that house. I encourage my son to get out of that house quickly. I also felt the pressure to remember the past. I know that there will be time for me to accept reality and move on.

However, he found his favorite toy and said, *"Oh! I found my dump truck, yeah, this is my dump truck toy when I was little."* DoctorSon picked up the dump truck and rolled on the steps going down and dragged it to the wall. When we were in the kitchen, he set the dump truck toy on the table and pushed all the way to wall towards me and said, *"watch out mommy, here's the dump truck coming," "Whew! I almost got hit."* I said with a smile on my face but deep inside in me was sadness. The memorable moments when our minds search for the past, whether happy and sad moments our body reacts to it.

I was almost on the edge when the marriage collapsed which inside the house, you can see the result of what's going on for the people living in it. I remembered, due to headache, I felt, I took 3 Tylenols in one time to stop the pain. Setting myself in the bedroom, got some glass full of water and took the medicine. My two sons, EldestSon and DoctorSon were on my side with my mother. I was so tired that night, and my children noticed why I didn't wake up that morning after the night of being sound asleep. My mother was there too, who would take care of my children if I were at work, was worried and wondering why I had not woken up that morning. But after I recovered and woke up my kids were aware of what had happened. Too tired of going through and reminiscing about the past. Being asleep for that moment is resting my mind of memories. I was then able to rethink and clear my mind through napping for a while.

It was painful memories that never be forgotten. Until I came back to the house with my 2 children the memories kept opening. Tears came from my eyes I felt warm on my face. The coldness of the house I can feel on my skin when memories lingered. My remembrance of memories in this house was disrupted when my DoctorSon was playing with the dump truck, his favorite toy. *"Brimmmm, brimmmmm, brimmmm, mommy watch out the dump truck is going down."* My DoctorSon said. I responded, *"Let's go kiddo, let's get out of here now, it's too cold in here. Come on, let's go home. Oh! Are we going to Burger King, mom?* DoctorSon asked. I said, *"Okay, let's go to Burger King!"* My son reminded me, *"Mommy, you forgot the mail in the mailbox".* I somehow try to get away from that house quickly with the feeling of coldness and painful memories I always run away from it. Although painful memories still exist at that moment, there is always hope within my mind that there will be a good life out there, somewhere, and I believe.

In the present time, as a published author, I didn't know what to subtitle of the next chapter of this book. One day I turned the television on and the word "The Trashing Floor" flashes in my very sight listening to Joel Olsteen one of my five favorite Christian Television broadcasters. The date was Sunday, May 31, 2015. The beginning of trashing floor experiences began in the year 1997 when we, my 2 children and I suffered with hunger and no heater in the winter. I could not be approved for food stamps and welfare due to my investment properties in Ocala Florida and living in a four-bedroom home with swimming pool in New Jersey it was difficult to get help from the welfare system. The difficulty was when a husband and wife disunite and disconnect, the children suffer the most. The marriage was not led by the heart, but by the mind. When there are children involved in the marriage, children suffer the most from this disunity of family.

My children and I were abandoned by Ex-Husband. I have 2 children to be fed. Followed by financial disarray and wiped out of resources, cash, job, and both incomes disappeared. That I may say, hunger and famine in America existed in every selective individual's household. Therefore, this type of hidden agenda of the hardworking individual is taboo based on my own experiences. When you have investments, good income, paying higher income tax at the end of the year, and living in a big house, then divorce happened resources will be divided to point with nothing left. It seemed like a hard worker in America cannot get help from the government when disaster comes to life like divorce, death, flooding, and sickness. Therefore, it is now visible so many quit working pretend they are disabled because they can get money from the government that way. In my book titled "Feudalistic Era in 21st Century" I will explain all these why for these selective individuals would rather be disabled than employed!

To continue, Ex-Husband was a soldier who travels all over the world. He travels to Korea, Germany, and many parts of the world. I used to travel with him with our children, but I quit traveling with him when we got to New Jersey from Hawaii due to my work responsibilities. One day when he came home, and our children greeted him with a sign on the top of the door to surprise him and we shouted a joyous word says, *"Welcome Home Dad"* and it was supposed to be a happy moment. But I can see in his eyes that he was not happy to be home. It took a while for me to discover that he has another life somewhere where I do not want to know about. He must figure out his issues of having an affair, and if he is willing to talk about it, I am willing to listen but instead silence and taboo was the answer that communication went down the drain.

In 1998, I met a man that somehow helped me and reminded me of my ups and downs in life. I came across the visualization of the ups and downs in my life that it can be my tools to see the past and learn from that past. Although, I got married with this man I met in 1998, after five years of synthesizing on what had happened, but it took years for me to make that decision to re-marry again to any man. I was influenced by this man and was determined to survive with my 2 boys as a single mother without source of income. Instead, this man, Thomas motivated me to continue my education. I did. I then learn these days to have time for myself, but there are times that I would say "it's too late my children now are grown up."

I must let it go so I can move on.

Today, every time I tap into these experiences of mine, I can't help to cry. I do believe that at that moment of our suffering of hunger and no heater in the winter were just shoveled under the rug that today the very moment writing the passage I can't help to bring tears in my eyes. It feels good to cry on the shoulder of a man who I have become my confidante, my previous husband, Thomas. Thomas, whom I met in 1998 and had been married for 22 years. I am blessed to have him in my life from the year 1998 to 2020. We had a good life together.

CHAPTER TWELVE

The Past & The Future: The Reminiscing Time

I attended my EldestSon's wedding on April 5, 2012. My EldestSon was a son of my first involvement with a man I met in 1970 when I was modeling clothes and at the same time still looking for extra income in Manila. I forced myself to work in the restaurant which I didn't' like because being just a waitress was not my plan in life. I want bigger than that. In that restaurant as my second job, I was waitressing and servicing customers coming to the restaurant. I met a man of course we call him in this book the "BreadWinnerMan." After getting to know each other in a very puzzling way, we lived together for more than 5 years.

In the country I was born, there was no divorce. BreadWinnerMan was married and supposedly to get divorced from his wife, but the divorce was not granted therefore, I must separate myself from him. I venture instead to the USA through BreadWinnerMan's effort for me to go abroad in year 1984. I was one of the contract workers of Chinese company, Lucky Company that has a branch in New York. Once I settled in the USA, I petition my EldestSon to come to USA in the year 1991 and he came to the USA while we were in Hawaii at that time. My EldestSon came to America with my mother. I petitioned my mother the same year I petitioned my EldestSon.

In April 2012 was my EldestSon's wedding. Now they have four boys who are my grandchildren. It was a time for self-searching, and putting the puzzle of my life together, and reminiscing from the past was to remember what had happened and to make sure the pattern will not repeat. I have met some of the past relatives I truly want to forget. I could not forget my past and the people who are involved with my children and perhaps my grandchildren are still in my mind to remember. Forgetting the past and moving forward is a productive action for me. Due to the painful past, I have encountered I tend to not remember what's on the plate that day. However, I accepted it without hesitation. I greeted most of them and I tried not to talk about it because it still lingered in my mind to those reminiscing days. Writing this Memoir, I must get into remembering the bits and pieces of my life at that moment of my EldestSon's wedding. This book titled, "The Memoir: The River of Life" The flow of the river going through many hustles and bustles is just like life's journey here on earth of plenty.

The story behind my EldestSon whom the father's name, we will call him in this book, the BreadWinnerMan. I was living with BreadWinner as a mistress in year 1978 to 1984. and I got pregnant in year 1982. We are living together secretly and silently for more than 6 years. With a luxurious life I had with him with maids, guard, and a driver I was mesmerized of my living situation. However, after living for how many years as we think as a luxurious life, I had come to a crashing halt as my mind kept thinking of my life was in imprisonment stage and I have no freedom. I then became paralyzed to a point where I couldn't do anything. I somehow could not function my mind was unable to create. I became so dependent, and I felt like I am becoming a disabled individual. I became miserable, depressed, suicidal, and dysfunctional; therefore, I cried all day and night long.

When EldestSon was only more than 2 years old I need to change my environment therefore, I decided and plan to get out of my luxurious lifestyle without thinking that I have 2 years old baby left behind in my country heading to the United States of America, the land of the free. Another part of me that was missing was my EldestSon was born in the month of October 1982, and I left him in year 1984.

First, I carried a baby with 7.9 pounds, and I am only a tiny women weight of 95 founds. When I had to be in the emergency to bore him, I had a C-section. Then after a month, I must go back to the hospital for emergency because the wound opened, I was bleeding. My maid called an ambulance. I was into postpartum depression. I was very sick and one of his nephews was there to help me. While I was healing, the maid was the one who took care of my son. Then, the feeling of guilt and shame living with a man who was married. I always remember my mother would say when I was young "No Sex Before Marriage."

In the month of April in the year 1984 I left him with my babysitter and flew to America. While I was working with Lucky Company in United States of America, devastation begins in my life being my EldestSon was left behind with my babysitter in the country. I was very distraught and sad. I then kept sending mail to my maid asking how he was doing. Next, I send a letter to my sister Nemie to come to my house there and take care of my EldestSon. However, I heard nothing from all the communication I sent.

While trying to reconnect with my EldestSon in the country where he was born, my babysitter and my sister Nemie were also there to assist to take care of him when I left to America. I just found out recently talking to my sisters through FaceTime, after all that his father, the BreadWinnerMan we call him, was realigning the house I used to live in and brought my son to his household near the manufacturing business he had. From then on, my son was with his father, the BreadWinnerMan, and HisWife.

He was taken care by a babysitter, and of course HisWife. Before, this realignment happened, HisWife went to the house where BreadWinnerMan bought for me to live in. She saw my sister Nemie which she thought that Nemie was me, the mistress of her husband, the BreadWinnerMan. HisWife visited the house I was living in, and knocked the door, and saw my sister Nemie at the door. HisWife went back to her car and picked up a gun heading towards my sister, Nemie. My maid came to the door, and both Nemie and my maid panicked at the threat of a gun pointing at her. Both explained to her that Nemie, my sister was not me. HisWife went back to her car and very agitated and angry. Nemie and my maid didn't know what had happened then in BreadWinnerMan's household. The next thing was my son was taken away, and the house I used to live in was empty and closed.

To continue, I petition my EldestSon to come to USA. In 1991, my EldestSon was 9 years old I picked him up at the airport. My mother was with him both came at the same time. I was trying to get to know my son, and him to know me, but there were issues between me and him. Something we could not agree on, such as some behavior I did not like, and I perfectly understood what he was going through without a biological mother, me, with him growing up. The struggles of my EldestSon and me, became worse.

In attending high school in the USA, he neglected his school, and his grades were not good as my goals for him were not fulfilled if grades in school were very low. I would receive letters from the school administration about the issues in school. I got worried about his grades. While we were in New Jersey after my divorce with my Ex-Husband in 1997, I struggled more, and my son and I kept fighting and it was not a healthy relationship as son and a mother. One of my Ex-HusbandCousin was trying to help me to temporarily adopt my EldestSon, so that I would have time with DoctorSon, my younger son, and to realign my life after divorce with my Ex-Husband. (Well, my EldestSon was the son of the BreadWinnerMan.) The goal was to finish his High School education to move forward to college. But it didn't go in that direction. My Eldestson was taking vocational school to be certified, not a degree education which was the Ex-HusbandCousin's decision, not mine.

One day, while writing this memoir, I was digging into the past and found a letter I wrote to my EldestSon's teacher about what's going on that I could not handle any more of my son's behavior and his attendance in school affected his grades. I gave up because it was not healthy for me and for him due to many fights all the time. Although, I felt bad being he had to live with someone's household, the ExHusband'sCousin household.

In addition, I signed a document with Ex-HusbandCousin that was not witnessed by a Certified Notary in front of me, and Ex-HusbandCousin. The documents I signed I found out after re-reading without rushing through reading and understanding the documents that the documents I signed were not legal at all. As a Notary Public in New Jersey and, at that time, finishing my education at a higher level, a PhDs in Human Services, the documents I signed I did not read while signing were not legal because documents were signed without witnesses by a Notary

Public. Also, after signing, I found out that the document I signed was about to adopt my EldestSon permanently, which was NOT my intention. My failure was that I did not read the document before signing, and my ignorance of the legality of the documents. Now that I have a PhDs. in Human Services and am a Notary Public in the States of New Jersey and now Florida, that transaction I had with my Ex-Husband'sCousin was NOT legal. The reason I am telling you this is that I do believe that these are the reasons why my eldest son, who, until these days, has not wanted to talk to me. It is difficult to explain this situation to my EldestSon. I'd rather give all these issues to the Lord, I thought, and I did. However, just lately, in the year 2023, I met all of my grandchildren from my EldestSon, and it was a wonderful journey for me.

Furthermore, I can't go back to the past and correct it. I do believe that it's too late. My EldestSon, already developed a non-communicative relationship with me. Although Ex-HusbandCousin's goal was to help me at that time in my life after the divorce of my Ex-Husband, this type of event had never been forgotten. A mother and son's relationship created a barrier due to the event in which I was innocent of signing a document I didn't know it was the purpose to adopt my son permanently. I tried my best to communicate and also he tried to put together the relationship between a mother and son, but I was not focused on it due to my many problems I had at that time such as divorce, filing child support, house is foreclosing, and financial was not achieved due to I quit my 2 jobs to have time and realign my life to the right direction or shall I say, a NORMAL way of living.

Today, and at the present time I visit children that are neglected and abused through Guardian Ad Litem program. I learned that by adopting a child at age 13 a foster parent gets $550.00 per child from the government here in Florida, I am not sure in Maryland and New Jersey. Putting the pieces together I now understand, monetary benefits that drive human beings although it affects the relationship between son and mother. At GALP, always that children must be returned to biological parents if there is no physical and psychological abuse in the family.

Since I was young, my dream was and is always been to be educated at a higher level. My younger son, whom we call "DoctorSon,". Is now a medical doctor. My dream was to go up to a higher level of education as my dream when I was very young was now fulfilled in my 50's and to this day. Education is to learn and gain more knowledge on things we like to know about. Our Thought Universe is huge and vague; therefore, education and educating yourself to a point where you are satisfied or may not go forward and learn and be educated to some points to help others. There are times that we must just let go of what we planned and goals, not be devastated when it's not fulfilled. I do believe that there must be a reason why it must have happened.

When we let go of things we cannot do, it somehow goes in the direction where we are supposed to have, and of course no stress and hardship because it just goes along the path that we are supposedly in. I learned that the hard way. Although, I do not have regret at all. I am thankful to the Lord that my life was and is guided by the Almighty, and I do believe since when I was young and to this day in my now 60s.

EldestSon met a woman and got married. She is now my daughter in law since in year 2012. As a result, they have four boys who are my grandchildren. Such a blessing! Although my Eldestson and I were distant from each other due to issues we had such as I left him in the country where he was born, and the situation I had there was totally difficult to comprehend for my son. I am thankful that he now settled with a stable family with his wife, a happy family. He is such a good father of his four boys and seems very happy and successful in life. Thank you, Lord.

However, on July 22, 2023, DoctorSon invited me to go to Orlando to see all my grandchildren heading to Disney World. My EldestSon, his wife, and my 4 grandsons; DoctorSon, his wife, and 2 grandchildren we ate together at Dimsum restaurant in Orlando, and it was the very best day of my life. I have my husband, Cameron, with us together all of us such a wonderful time, my tears fell on my cheek as a feeling of gratitude. Again, deep inside of me I am thankful to the Lord. While reading this paragraph, my husband,

Cameron, and I have tears of gratitude. I got married with Cameron in November 2022, and this is the first he met my EldestSon.

Remembering when my DoctorSon was 8 years old at that time, he was struggling to be fatherless. DoctorSon was born in 1987 in Germany. His father is my Ex-Husband, whom I married in the year 1985 and divorced in 1997. After a year or two, I met a man. Having a new man in my life at that time, who became my children's stepfather named Thomas, seemed like a new living situation for my children at that time. Living with Thomas (my husband at that time, who passed away in the year 2020) was a new environment for my two children. In the year 1998, Thomas and I got married. It lasts for a period of 22 years. On December 17, 2020, Thomas passed away.

My son, DoctorSon, got married to his Wife in the the year 2016, and currently, they have 2 children, a boy and a girl, who are my grandchildren. I visited them more often than the children of my EldestSon because they live nearby the distance was not an issue. My eldest son was married to his wife with now 4 boys, who are my grandchildren. I have realized that when a husband and wife are disunited, children are hurt, and some are lost in the process of growing.

Therefore, family unity is impossible to recover. Perhaps growing up goes in a different direction in life, and we can find a new way of living. It could be for better or for worse or perhaps in between. I have never experienced this type of family disunity of husband and wife while I was growing up. My parents always stayed together and never separated. In the country where I was born, rules and regulations are ***no divorce, no sex before marriage, family unity must be intact, and respect for the elderly.*** Therefore, I do believe in husband-and-wife unity, and family members' connectivity for the sake of relationship and bonding must be intact for family unit and relatives. This type of unity has given the family unity strength, bonding ability, and strength between family members. Also, family members help one another, and there is no reliance on government money and food stamps.

I remember growing up, family bonding helps one another, and that's why I put my nieces and nephews to school and am still able to help my family, although I have been away from them for more than 35 years now. For me, the bond is still there. Although growing up, there were disagreements and discontent in relationships between some of my sisters, bonding still exists in that form, somehow. Although we are far from each other with no connection then, now, in the digital world, there will always be connectivity.

When husband and wife do not connect at the beginning of marriage due to responsibilities to travel around the world, however, there will be a disconnection, and somehow relationship does not grow into becoming a healthy family unit. I have noticed that today's Generation X is now changing to a different direction of life, the "Isolation Phenomena" of the new generation or perhaps from the past, making it now visible to all.

In year 1997 feeling of being alone, and family unity somehow did not develop strongly when I got divorced from Ex-Husband, the father of DoctorSon, I somehow was relieved of something, something I did not understand. The divorce process somehow has given me the freedom, and opportunity to move forward. I still asked the question until these days as if "I lost my feeling of being married because Ex-Husband travelled all over the world, and somehow the feeling of being a wife was not developed. It declined along the way somehow. Our togetherness in Germany and Hawaii while we were traveling with him somehow was not enough to put the unity of marriage. It got lost somewhere due to time spent working to earn income.

At that time, I learned that when husband and wife are far away from one another, development of relationship fades away. The divorce process was easier. Secondly, after knowing of him having an affair, I totally lost interest in our relationship. Also, when he withdrew $2,000.00, he gave to his uncle was shocking to me. I was then the one who paid the 7 overdrawn checks in the bank where I used to work, the Credit Union in New Jersey.

Although I worked in the Bank of Credit Union, I still had to pay off the checks overdrawn due to my Ex-Husband's secret withdrawal of $2,000. It was a $35 per check fee for an overdrawn account. It was the end of our relationship. I could not accept this type of family unit where there were so many secrets. Although it was a painful past in my life because my children were involved, it was my worry and concern for my children not to have a stable family. It was an overwhelming feeling of sadness at that time. That's why I would cry for that reason. However, I managed it anyway. The Lord was and is always with me. I do believe.

Although I found another man in my life in 1998, life always goes in a different direction. Due to the struggles of our living situation, I must have someone with me, I thought. My new man in my life at that time, Thomas, comforted me and was with me all the way through my struggles as a single mother. He had given me a place to live with my 2 young children. Being with Thomas from 1998 to 2020, we had a good life together. But, of course, there were agreements and disagreements between ideas. We somehow manage our differences along the way. However, when Thomas passed away on December 17, 2020, the grieving was too intense. It took a very long time for me to recover from the grieving period, and the pain continues until these days; grieving in some moments still exists.

I could not release myself from grieving. I constantly cry every morning at 2 A.M. all the way. The pain and suffering of

Thomas's passing were still in my mind. I felt like half of my life was taken away. While grieving for the loss of my previous husband, I am the only one taking care of the house that got flooded on September 16, 2020. I got lost in my life journey here on earth of plenty. I had no one to release all my suffering inside, but only to pray to God to help me with these struggles I am in. I couldn't see the Lord within my struggles in the beginning, but now I see. The Lord was with me all the way, but I couldn't see Him then.

I could remember that I always played the song by Zack Williams and Dolly Parton, *There Was Jesus.* However, this was only after I had been through all the way. I was so thankful for all the determination to pray and being positive that from "darkness, there is light." Yes. There is light after darkness, and I've learned a lot about the many challenges I have been through in life. My experiences have given me the knowledge on how to survive in the time of my life journey in darkness. I truly became stronger and more skillful. I am very thankful for all the struggles I've been through. It may sound questionable when I say, "I am thankful for all the struggles I went through," but you will understand when you are in it. You will see.

Again, Thomas and I have lived together as a married couple from 1998 through December 2020. In the grieving period of his passing in the year 2020, I felt like something was missing in my life for 22 years, just gone and disappeared. The feeling of emptiness and aloneness I somehow can't take it in. I went to hide in my room where I could release all the many pains and suffering in my life. I felt like something was missing in my life journey here on earth of plenty. We used to dance, sing karaoke, watch movies, and do some work on our lawn being together with one another. Now that he is gone, I feel empty, alone, and lonely, and something is missing kind of feeling. A wonderful experience that can't be forgotten in time. We share ideas with one another that gave us more knowledge in life together.

We as humans have many different ideas, and sharing with our partner in life could be a blessing and create abundance in life. I called this sharing the contents of the Thought Universe that makes us more skillful and knowledgeable of things we didn't have and knowing the unknown. Our stages in life have given us many experiences in many ways in which each one of us may differ. Either we accept it based on positivity and to benefit our well-being such a good Knowledge Sharing, ourselves becomes abundant in knowledge from others who we may not know about.

In the beginning, Thomas and I became business partners together, and it progressed to companionship and free spirit in my regard. I went further than that in my part while continuing my education to a higher level. I was able to fly higher in my endeavor in life. Thomas's support and motivation helped me through furthering my higher level of education, PhDs. Living here in the

USA, the land of the free, my father says America is heaven. Since I was a child, I have fulfilled my dreams and become true as being educated to a higher level of education: Doctor of Philosophy, major in Human Services in Management and Leadership.

I chose this major because my interest is to help children who are neglected and abused in the family. Also, I have now become an entrepreneur due to the education I have accumulated. I retired now, enjoying my life with my husband, Cameron, whom I married in November 2022. I enjoyed being with Cameron, and we traveled all over the United States of America. And we plan to travel internationally while continuing my book writing. Thank you, Lord. Amen. I am always thankful for all I have, whether small or big. It does not matter, but what matters is we are so abundant in life, and we are provided, but most of us cannot recognize that. I am thankful for every little and big thing that happened in my life because I have RECOGNIZED God's given abundance and blessings. That's the reason I am THANKFUL for it.

CHAPTER THIRTEEN

Being A Business Minded To Be A Self-Employed

What did I do and how did it happen? Anyway, I could not go back to the past, but instead in my mind I gathered some ideas on how to escape from a nightmare I was in where my children were involved. That's breaking my heart. That week, I spoke to my children and asked them what they wanted to do after school. I told my children that my friend Sol told me about the Flea Market. I have no idea what a Flea Market was. I asked my friend Sol if there's lot of fleas in that market. She said to me with a smile that Flea Market means, the vendors can go anywhere they want. Meaning, it's like a flea can jump to any place where they can find food. I said to my friend Sol, surprisingly *"what is a name and its meaning? Flea Market."* I was amazed of the name, *"Flea Market."*

I then gathered my children at the age of 8 and 13, and we had a meeting about building a business at Flea Market. I suggested if they want to sell something at flea market to earn income, we can move from one place to another like fleas. They can choose what they want to sell at Flea Market. My children were excited to do something to sell for earning income. However, I do not have cash or money to buy merchandise to sell. Besides, I do not know where flea market is located at that time, and I do not know how to do this type of business. My friend Sol guided me where to go. I met Sol at the church and trained me where to go and how to get a table at the flea market. She told me that there is a flea market in Collingswood, New Jersey and it is only $5 per table. I said that's not bad for the price of the table.

I started thinking about what to sell for the children to enjoy and at the same time earning a little income. I went to the welfare system to ask for help, but I was denied but suggested that I can borrow $475 and must pay it once I earned income. I agreed and that money I bought merchandise to sell at the flea market, the figurines. I spent $300 for those figurines and other stuff, collectable stuff. So, I was able to provide merchandise for my children to sell. Although we were struggling, we were excited to set up at Flea Market to try a new adventure for this type of business. However, that Friday morning at 8 am, it rained. Three of us were staring at the window and feeling sad because we may not be able to sell our merchandise that day because of the rain. Three of us were praying at the window looking up in the sky talking to the Lord up there. I somehow became a child at that moment, and I forgot all the suffering I felt deep inside. Then after praying we hugged each other.

At around 9:00 in the morning I checked the weather outside and found out the rain had stopped. I told my children with enthusiasm and smiles that the sun came up and it shines so brightly, and the rain stopped. In my mind, the rain is just passing through just like our situation of hunger and famine. Exactly like a river that it goes high and low then floods then calming down. I always see the spiritual vision on where life is going and how it goes. My children jumped to joy, and we prayed for the rain to be gone totally, and it did. Three of us were jumping to joy. We were so happy that the Lord heard our prayer. I told my children to get ready and let's go. We did. We were singing along to the way heading to Flea Market at Collingswood New Jersey. It's an hour drive to get there coming from Bayville, New Jersey and finally we got there, and I went to the office to pay the table and $5 was our last cash.

Our table was situated across the office entrance, and the one on the left side of the entrance door a businessman selling pants, and shirts situated across us was perfect for me to see and find out and I am learning what to do at the flea market by watching people selling stuffs there. I focused watching this man selling pants and shirts because he somehow selling it fast, and I see the activities of his table. He is putting money in his pocket and wrapping merchandise in a plastic bag fast enough to put cash in his pocket.

I was watching this man constantly to learn his technique. Of course, I must wear my dark sunglasses not to be seen that I am watching this man across my table selling his merchandise fast. So many questions in my mind on how to be in business like this man who constantly putting cash in his pocket from the sale of his merchandise. I am now thinking of asking him a question of where he buys those pants and shirts able to sell it for very less price? Maybe I can compete with him, I thought. However, I couldn't even say hello and or say hi to this man because I feel embarrassed and reluctant to meet another man in my life due to my experiences.

In the meantime, a man selling hotdogs passing by was reminiscing my merchandise and was talking to me while I was watching the man selling shirts and pants. My eyes kept watching the man who was selling his merchandise so quickly, and at the same time paying attention of the man selling hotdog. I asked the guy selling hotdog how much the hotdog was. I need to feed my children. I also introduced my children to the hotdog guy, and somehow, he had conversation with my children. I was worried about what to feed my children that day while at the flea market, not selling my merchandise yet. I told this hotdog man that I do not have money to pay him for the hotdog. He can come back later to get the payment. He said not to worry about paying him. This man gave hotdogs to my two boys to eat for lunch for free and I was relieved. I gave thanks to this hotdog guy while watching the man across my table on how and where this man got his merchandise to sell it so cheap and able to gain more profit.

By the way, I had my sunglasses on so this man was unable to recognize that I was watching him perhaps I will be accused of eye stalking, and he might think I have a crush on him. I was just amazed at how he could just have this business going and money in the pocket so quickly. The people are buying his merchandise non-stop. While staring at this man I saw two customers stealing merchandise. Somehow, he didn't even care, he continued servicing his customers, putting the shirt and pants sold in the bag and putting money in his pocket. I was the one who worried that his merchandise would be stolen. Suddenly, these two customers went back and paid the man for the shirt/pants they stole and three of them laughed. Later, I saw three of them went inside the building and had some coffee.

I then figured out that they are friends and knew each other. In my mind, I would like to get to know this man and ask where he buy his merchandise. I am thinking to compete with this man selling and become a business owner and his competitor. However, I was a little shy to approach a man about that issue. I just pretended that I was not watching him and at the end of that day, he came to my table and asked me if I wanted to have coffee with him. My dark sunglasses didn't work as good as I thought. Of course, I said yes. In my mind, finally I will find out where he buys these shirts and pants that he could sell for a very less price. People are buying. Amazing!

We went to Red Lobster restaurant and ate dinner, not just coffee. While heading to the restaurant, I was asking lots of questions about his merchandise, and he could not answer all my questions. He was just listening and listening, and I must stop asking because there was no answer coming from him. I only heard him saying, uhmmm, uhmmmm, and at the same repeated my question such as "where do you buy these merchandises you sell at the Flea Market? He would answer me like this *"Where do I buy the merchandise, I sell at the flea market…ahaaa, ahaaa."* But my questions are more than answers. I must stop asking questions and let him answer me one question at a time. He said to me, *"I will take you to the place where I buy my merchandise if you want."* I answered him with excitement, *"Of course I want you to bring me there."* And he responded, *"aha…okay, great!"* I was so happy. Finally, my plan to compete with him will be fulfilled.

So, one day, he called me and asked me if I wanted to go with him to Pennsylvania to the manufacturing of shirts and pants. I said a big YES. It was Monday, and he would come to pick me up at my house. He asked for my address and of course I gave it to him. He lives in Bricktown, and I live in Bayville, it's only 30 minutes' drive from his house to my house. So, he came, and I was riding in his old van with lots of merchandise in the back. I looked at the merchandise and somewhere still in boxes. He asked me if I was hungry, and if we could eat lunch before or after. I was hungry at that time because the food I had saved was for my children when they came home from school. So, I said, yes, we can eat lunch, thank you. My stomach was filled with real food instead of noodles.

We finally came to our destination, and I saw this big building. We parked in the back, and we just went inside without even asking permission from whoever was there. He continued going upstairs and I just followed him, and he said hello to one of the workers, and I waved my hand only with a smile. The area was huge and full of shirts and pants. These are the rejects in the manufacturing that when a shirt is made and counted also a small damage is called *"reject"* and they would isolate this *"reject"* merchandise and sell it for very cheap. The damage part cannot be seen. It is so tiny that sometimes it's hard to see. Now I understand why it is so cheap, and he was able to sell it for a very cheap price. I got it now. I am learning, I thought.

Once a week we go to these manufacturing buildings and buy those merchandise and sell it at the Flea Market every Friday, Saturday, and Sunday. Every Monday we visit these places, and Tuesday I ended up helping him sort out those merchandise, and Wednesday and Thursday we go motorcycling. I enjoyed our company together that we ended up developing an intimate relationship of each other instead of competition in business to sell the same merchandise. It didn't go towards that direction for me to have a business like his because we ended up having an affair as lovers, but not to appoint to have sexual intimacy before marriage. Don't give me wrong, but temptation was always there. *I always see my mother's face angry and saying, "No sex before marriage"* with a pointed finger wiggling in front of me. However, it was just within my Thought Universe.

Although, it took months and a year to really developed our relationship, a forever relationship I had with this man, Thomas, my previous husband at that time   was worth being with this man, a loving man with compassion and integrity. Thomas passed away on December 17, 2020, we had great memorable moments and unity as husband and wife for 22 years together.

In year 1998 I had to file child support from Ex-Husband whom I married in the year 1986 in New Orleans, the father of my son, DoctorSon. Thomas (whom I met in year 1998 was helping me with how to process child support from Ex-Husband. Thomas helped me with everything I pursue in my life such as my higher education as a PhDs, and I also helped him on having another business ventures such as I trained him to be a mortgage closer, and signer. We then opened a limousine business, and I am the person who was behind him to do marketing, paper works, and office activities of the business. We became united and able to help and support one another of any kind, that after so many years of selling merchandise at Flea Market we ended up looking for ways on another types of venture while I am continuing my higher education from AA Degree at Brookdale Community College, in 2000-2002, Batchelor's degree at Georgian Court University in year 2003-2004. He started driving trucks to haul dirt, limousine business, and I trained him on how to do mortgage signing or closing as my self-employed type of work while continuing my education in a higher level.

One day I sometimes go with Thomas if I am not in school, or I do not have mortgage closing assignment that day. We went to this huge land of dirt, and I was so amazed by the area I have never been before. I wrote a short story with rhyming words in school as part of my assignment from my undergrad, AA degree majored in Literature doubled with Photography as part of my writing assignment, a short story I have created of this place where he took me was a memorable moment being with him at that time. My first experience being in a huge truck where I can see everyone from a higher level. I then wrote a poetic memorable passage that was made into a rhyming form of life experience expression. (See below).

"A Lady On The Red Soil"

Once my grandfather said, "little girl on the red soil" Until now what he meant was a puzzle to me. That was then when I was five years old, but just recently, I recalled after seeing this place—to me, it is desirable…Staying in the house, one day, I got bored, I decided to go with my husband Thomas, riding in his big dump truck to load soil and stones. We went to a place where a huge truck goes. Opening this big door in his big dump truck I found that the door was too heavy. Lifting my left leg to get up on ladder, I hung on the handle of the truck door lifting my right leg was difficult for me to accomplish. When we were on the highway, I felt like I was the highest, biggest tallest person among all. I could see people in their cars, and I could see them all.

Further down the road of quiet driving, we were about to enter the gate of Millington Stone Quarry. Here we came to a big, huge empty space on earth. "Holly! Molly! Guacamole! I spoke. Amazed, the place I have never seen. We never knew that there were desirable places hidden. Maybe, you too-can find a similar place around, for you it maybe, silly as it may sound.

The Millington Stone Quarry was the place. Well, I would say it was odd for me because I never saw such a huge terrain before. From the surface it was about three hundred deep of carved land. Every corner and side by side carved like small steps on the side of the mountain. You will see the different colors for the soil. At the front side when you drive in you will see the carved-in land formed like an open paper cliff. Inside, against the wall of carved land, there are different colors of soil. In every side of the land mixed colors with dark brown, black, orange, red, light brown, yellow and gray. I visualized the different colors and remembered my grandfather used to call me "little girl on the red soil.

It processed through my thought and still vivid in my mind when I was five years old, I used to stand up in small gathered red soil made by ants (ants' house). I jumped on it and squeezed my feet on the red soil to make my feet colored in red. Thank God, ants went to get some food for rainy days. I also danced and sang, waved, squeezed red soil with my bare hands. That's why my grandfather called me "little girl in the red soil.

Not knowing when I was a child and seeing this place related to it amazed me, and it was appreciated. Now, down here, I am watching these huge trucks inside this nicely unintended landscaped place, three hundred feet hole, big trucks go in to be loaded with soil and bring it to another place. When you see these huge trucks from a far distance, they look like toy trucks, but these are real, big, huge trucks in the near distance. Is this place desirable? For me, based on my routine then, going to school, going home and work, I think this place is a very interesting place and sights to see compared to different places from what you've seen every day. Finally, if you feel like you need a vacation, look around your area; there might be some places you never knew existed.

Like natural resources surround your neighborhood, it might be a desirable place. Now, it reveals all that is, just what my grandfather says, "little girl on the red soil" becomes "lady on the red soil" at this place where you can see different colors of soil, you will be amazed. Uncovered the long, long-ago story from my grandfather, now became history.

From what I understood about humanity based on my experiences, we are in many different colors living here on earth of plenty, enjoying the beauty of many colors of humanity; we learned the many different types of beauty and cultures mixed. We learned what's best for each one of us as humans living in a temporary here in this world while heading on our journey in life to where we are supposed to be. Treasuring the experiences I have in life made me more capable of adapting to the reality of life and very easy to move forward, giving me strength and peace of mind.

This experience I have with Thomas, my previous husband for 22 years, will never be forgotten. Reconnecting my past when my grandfather says, "little girl in the red soil" which through riding with Thomas's huge truck to pick up dirt, I was so amazed, and my grandfather remembrance was reopened and remembered. Now, it is so amazing how our lives reconnect to someone where no longer living here on earth of plenty, but still exist in a very different form, the memory. Living for 22 years as a married couple with Thomas from 1998 to 2020 was so much appreciated. While I am living here on earth, he will not be forgotten. I filed a lawsuit for the rehab where my previous husband was confined due to negligence in the organization's part.

Although I won the case, I was still grieving of his passing. Therefore, counseling continues even until I find someone. I am somehow unable to live by myself. It seems something is missing living alone. As being a widow since year 2020 to 2022 there are many men that I have encountered but I avoided them all. I thought I am still married to my previous husband Thomas whom I married for 22 years who passed away in year 2020 and join with the Lord in heaven, I do believe.

My counselor's advised me to let Thomas go and he is now in the hands of the Almighty. God's guidance is on my way now and is always since then. The many trials in my life since then I had overcome them all. I felt like I am the winner with God's guidance. I am always the winner walking in this world of plenty. Through my life journey, like a river of life I always saved myself from the ups and downs of the water flowing, and perhaps toward flooding that creates worse scenario of the river of life. The many trials in my life begins when we got flooded in by Sally Hurricane in September 16, 2020.

CHAPTER FOURTEEN

The Many Trials In My Life:
But I Am Still Standing

In the beginning, it was a beautiful and moving forward kind of lifestyle when my previous husband, Thomas and I moved from New Jersey to Panhandle Florida in year 2004. While continuing my education to master's degree in online Majored in Human Resources Management with University of Phoenix, and continually moving to higher education in Doctor of Philosophy (PhDs), I opened businesses in Panhandle Florida. My businesses were doing so great, however when Covid came, flood, sickness, and death I went through everything fall apart again. When Sally Hurricane, COVID-19 came to our area and most of my businesses were closed, such as Bonifay Guild for the Art, Inc 501 C3 nonprofit organization I designed and formed in 2005, Notarial assignments in mortgage closing, signing, solemnize marriages, art, and book signing. In year September 16, 2020, our house got flooded by Sally Hurricane. It was up to my chest the water coming from the broken busted levy in the neighboring area. That day and for 2 weeks my husband at that time, Thomas, and I lived in hotels and motels for a while until we found a vacant apartment in Dothan Alabama. Living in the hotel for more than a month was very costly.

Although it is far from where our property got flooded but we must rent it. It was the only apartment available in the area nearby. It takes 45 minutes travel from the new apartment to our house that got flooded. We settled down in Dothan from October 2020 to December 2020. I started the flood insurance processes for the house to be renovated. I would come back and forth while my previous husband, Thomas (with Parkinson, and dementia) was with me wherever I go. I would arrange for him to sit in the passenger seat. Heading to our house that got flooded I am always the driver since when he was suffering from dementia. Our activities had changed and shifted in a different direction in life.

I can't forget the moments when my previous husband, Thomas, and I fell on the ground because he was shaking while him and I walked towards the car to go to his doctor's visit appointment. He was about to collapse, and I tried my best to prevent that movement and I ended up on the ground and he was on top of me. I had my head hit on the ground, and he broke one of his ribs, according to the doctor. I was suffering from a head injury and had taken Tylenol for the pain, and he was also in pain when he started moving that affected his broken rib. I am only 4 feet 11 weight of 109 and he was 5 feet 11 height with weight of 180. Because of the weight and height difference between my previous husband, Thomas, and I, I became vulnerable and failed to protect him. Both of us got injured but I was cured more quickly than him. I was then able to oversee him every minute of the day.

I would situate him to sit down on the sofa to watch TV for me to be able to take care of household responsibilities. After household responsibilities, I would give him activities such as body movements, dancing slow exercise, walking back and forth from the kitchen to the bathroom and living room. Also, he wants to be active in cleaning the car. There were times that I must watch him due to his inability to reach out of things that he needed, and if he missed a step he would fall. I would dress him up, but he wanted to do it himself, and I agree but I must watch him to make sure he does it without falling.

I was constantly watching him and sometimes when I had a problem with one of my tenants, I must bring him with me to constantly watch him. Also, I felt better that I could see him while I was doing my everyday household responsibilities. Although I was stressed out but the most important was to take care of my previous husband that had Parkinson and dementia.

One day, early in the morning I got up at 3 o'clock to continue editing my manuscript and I settled in the living room, and he was by himself in our bedroom sleeping on bed. At five am he got up and went to the bathroom. Usually, it is always at 6 am when he gets up and goes to the bathroom and I will assist him to the bathroom. I had my clock set up at 5:45 am. However, he got up earlier than I thought. I heard a thug sound and groaning. I stood up right away and checked our bedroom and he was on the bathroom floor bleeding. I called 9-1-1 right away, and while talking to the 9-1-1 representative I was crying that unable for the 9-1-1 representative to understand what I was saying.

The 9-1-1 representative tried to calm me down. While Thomas was in pain, and I couldn't take it that I panicked more. After how many minutes six emergency crew came and knocked on the door, and I was able to open the door with cellphone on my ear and was panicking and crying. I am so thankful for the Dothan Alabama emergency team. They were very efficient and fast. Thank you. It was then that Thomas was taken to Flower Hospital. Starting almost at the end of November 2020 my previous husband, Thomas, was confined at Flower Hospital in Dothan Alabama.

After many weeks, the doctor recommended that Thomas be put into rehab for leg healing; Thomas's children and I were debating on that situation because I did not agree, and my previous husband, Thomas, did not want to be in rehab due to some kind of abuse in that type of facility. Although Thomas has Parkinson's and dementia, he was still capable of making decisions of his own and had a good understanding of what was going on. There were times that he forgot things, but he was doing great at his age, at 86 years old.

Deciding on this issue to have Thomas confined at the rehab was very stressful because of fights, and disagreements between his grownup children, and I. The disagreement was about where to put Thomas in the rehab. I am sure that Thomas would not like to be in the rehab because of what's going on these days about rehab's negligence of residence in their facility. However, I would say, the doctor's advice to put him in the rehab and his grown-up children's decisions were followed instead of what I knew about my previous husband's request not to be in the rehab. I am torn apart in those moments of decision making what needs to be done based on Thomas' request when he was still in common sense stage of mind.

Covid 19: My Businesses Collapsed:

In year 2004, moving from New Jersey to Panhandle Florida was a different environment for me and my family. Looking for a job was a challenge. While taking my master's degree in human resource management, I was able to open a business a nonprofit organization, Bonifay Guild for the Arts, Inc, a 501 C3. I then continue my doctoral degree in Management and Leadership in Human Services through Capella University. I somehow accumulated and created organizations from being a Notary Public. Then I also opened an organization in the community, an Art Gallery that offered art display for all artists in the area and neighboring areas. My art Studio offers art classes, art supplies and many more such as note cards from the artist's original painting. I gathered more than 89 members. I had volunteers helping me manage these organizations while fulfilling my mortgage closing and signing to my clients at their residence.

Using my knowledge from higher education in Management and Leadership in Human Services as my hands-on training while continuing my PhDs at Capella University. I used my created businesses as my hands-on experiences using the thesis, lecture, research, and dissertation I must do when I was taking my masters and continuing to my doctoral programs. When Covid 19 came in our lives in year 2020 to these days while writing this manuscript the activities of my businesses changed dramatically, in addition to sickness and death of Thomas, my life turned in a very devastating direction. All my businesses were closed. More devastations begin in my life, while taking care of Thomas at the same time. On December 16, 2020, my previous husband, Thomas passed away.

Sally Hurricane On September 16, 2020

Another issue I must fulfill at that time of my grieving is to continue the renovation of our house that got flooded by Sallie Hurricane on September 16, 2020. Therefore, the renovation of the house got started after interviewing and choosing the reasonable cost of rebuilding our house. Interviewing builders was very exhausting. Finally, our gardener Mark found, or shall I say recommended Tommy, who became our builder to rebuild our house that got ruined by Sally Hurricane in the year 2020. Mark referred this builder to us which the quote was cheaper than any other builder I had interviewed. After how many days the renovation begins. I was visiting the renovation process to see how it was going but while I was in the car, I saw my builder, Tommy, with his workers. I asked so many questions about Tommy partly also to interview of who they were. Once I asked a question, he would answer me with a respect such as "Yes Ma'am." I somehow like his respectful manner.

On September 16, 2020, Sally Hurricane created havoc in our area. We got flooded and the damage was too extreme. My businesses closed, our lives changed dramatically from peaceful retirement to chaos, distraction, sickness, and death. Our lives transformed into something we have never been before, and the life transformation was so huge that while taking care of my previous husband, Thomas who struggled with Parkinson, and dementia it was exhausting to both of us. In addition, the flooding situation problems while taking care of him had given me the end of the line. I felt like falling apart again. While writing this page I can't help to cry. The memories are just too overwhelming that until these days while writing this Memoir since the flood it has been more than a year now but still fresh in my mind.

The Sallie Hurricane created havoc in our lives mentally and physically. My memory of the ones we processed through it was very stressful, life threatening, and very depressing. I may be able to explain here in this book how we are affected by this tragedy to be aware of next time when a disaster comes within our lives. I learned not to be drawn to it but instead learned to first save lives not only just the physical beings but also mentally. I once lived after that disaster, but not again to be taken my mental being to be depressed and stressed.

I could remember my previous husband with so many worries that our main house got flooded. I can see in his eyes of so many worries that I know he was not functioning well while living through it for how many months then he died. His eyes I can read and see the result of worries and stresses. I kept telling him not to worry and it would be okay. My calming behavior didn't work. I would hug him and cry with him, but I think that added to his worries. A man's mind is always with placing his woman to comfortable situation. However, in his situation where he could not do anything due to his Parkinson and dementia, he thinks he was unable to fulfill his goal to make me comfortable in life with him. I kept saying to him, "no worries" everything is well taken care of.

I do believe that these worries and stresses also brought him in the direction of dying. His body can't handle so many worries and stresses of course the Bonifay Rehab was part of his departing here on earth of plenty. He passed away on December 17, 2020. The Bonifay Rehab did not have workers to take care of him while he was in their care. He falls many times that it was the time for him to rest his tired body, and mentally exhausted of so much chaos in this world of plenty. These processes of exhaustions here on earth had taken my healthy mind and heart to many fights between living or dying. I, myself, was very sick due to these fights I had to survive.

First, it was obvious through my physical body losing so much weight, and not eating meals due to loss of appetite. While watching my previous husband going through dying, I can't help myself to sob, and cry to the highest level of mourning while he was still living due to what I am seeing while he was breathing so hard. It seemed he was suffering to maintain his life here on earth of plenty. Although, I would hide in the other room to cry. I was trying to accept the darkest of life.

Through breathing and crying I tried to release the pain I had encountered. This way I could survive the events of my life at that moment. I must release it all to keep me breathing and force my physical body and mind to keep moving., and at the same time to breathe, and breathe more to survive the pain I am encountering. It took months and years for me to calm the pain I've been in. The mourning and grieving were exhausting so my son recommended for me see a counselor to slow down the process of my body and mind through deterioration. Previously, before Thomas passed away, he suffered so much in this world of plenty to keep his life intact and to keep alive.

Sickness: Parkinson, Dementia, And Death

To continue when Thomas, my previous husband, was alive my journey with him was enjoyable. I enjoyed his company. We dance, sing and we tell stories from our past, mostly I would listen to his story because it interests me because he is much older than me. He is 23 years older. He was born in year 1934, and I was born in year 1957. I am learning about the era in his younger years in comparison to my generation as a baby boomer, and the new generation of today. I always record him when he tells story. I was unaware that he is preparing to leave me that day of December 17, 2020. Through his struggles to survive from falling first at the house early in the morning and was sent to emergency at Flower Hospital in Dothan near our apartment we temporarily lived, although recovered but again fell again twice at the rehab center in Bonifay.

After so many days in the hospital he was ready for rehab to supposedly strengthen his knees. However, the second and the third falls he could not survive. He suffered from so many falls. In addition, devastation from the flooding by Sallie Hurricane, and he was suffering from Parkinson, and dementia. My life went in a different direction, more darkness. While going through devastation in my life, I tried to analyze the situations.

The Rehab has no nurses at night to take care of him. He fell on the floor crawling naked to his roommate to ask for help. The next morning, he fell again in the bathroom. No one was helping him. When he was admitted in the rehab, I must wait for 10 days before I could visit him due to Covid situation at that time. I was not there for him, and no one took care of him at night. It was very devastating to know no one was there to take care of him which the most he needs help due to Parkinson, and dementia.

Again, he was confined to an emergency room. This event in his life was too much. It is also too much for me to accept the reality of what's going on. It is making me very sick. I struggled and blamed the Lord for what I am going through and asked the Lord "why me." The question I have, the Lord did not answer. In silence, I cried alone that affected my health. Writing these experiences of mine my tears comes out from my eyes like water dripping. I feel alone and devastated. Although, there are calls I received from relatives, the devastation was too much that I sometimes screamed to release all pressure within me. My life has changed dramatically. I could not eat, and I am losing weight so much that I must see a doctor due to my unhealthy habit such as forgetting to eat. I became anemic and lost so much weight. I surrendered and prayed instead. I prayed and prayed for the Lord to guide me in this very sad moment in my life.

While our house was in the process of renovation, I prepared myself by getting up in the morning to make phone calls to process the renovation of our home, flood insurances, and many paper works, despite the grieving period of my life, I must get up and move forward. The heaviness of my activity every morning dragged me down to the floor standing up by myself to survive, which no one knows. The struggles were so huge that I could not eat again. I was unable to move forward. I started crying louder and louder. I screamed to myself that after falling apart and cried so much, I fell asleep on the floor by myself. Due to pride, I could not tell anyone. However, my son notices my physical being seems unhealthy. My DoctorSon, the physician, recommended me to see a counselor, Dr. Simpson. I then continued seeing a counselor for many months. After how many months seeing a counselor, I feel normal and thinking I am now able to move forward. I hope that the darkness in my life will end soon. I thought that there would always be an end of darkness in life here on earth, and Thomas would not be forgotten.

Previously, before it all happened when we got flooded, Thomas couldn't drive the car anymore, according to his doctor. Thomas always comes with me when I do my job, Mortgage Closing and Signing. He could not drive anymore due to his Parkinson and dementia since year 2018. He also had a degenerative disease and was operated on. Therefore, for all the things that happened to him, he was limited in many activities, the things he used and liked to do. So, I am the one who handled everything that needed to be done in the house and other responsibilities in the house plus to take care of him. Besides, having a handyman, I only hire a handy man if I needed. Thomas passed away on December 17th, 2020, after his 86th birthday on December 11th. 2020. Thomas was confined to emergency services six times after all these falling from the hospitals, and the rehab.

When Thomas was in bed dying, I was also dying myself by forgetting to eat and without eating I had an episode of fainting, and I was losing so much weight. I felt like I was already dying while I was still alive. At that moment of my suffering, Thomas was in the process of dying. We all gathered including his children who came to visit their dad. I was devastated by my situation that I was crying everyday all day long that it affected my health. I see him struggling to breathe, and his children recommended to call the doctor for him not to continue his suffering by taking some medication to numb the pain. I disagree, but I was not on myself at the time. His children made the decision for his medication to numb the pain. Numbing the pain to his death that is. A medicine to stop breathing and I totally disagree with the decision of his children. However, I was not able to make the right decision at that moment due to my mentality was also corrupted due to many disastrous events came to my life. I left ignored the conversation we had with his grownup children, and I hid in my bedroom instead. Within 45 minutes after him taking the medication, his children called to come out from the bedroom I was hiding. His children told me to say goodbye to Thomas. I disagreed, and they explained to me why I need to say goodbye. I then obeyed their command although I did not understand what's going on.

The last of his breath was when I kissed him and said to him "It's okay my dear let it go, I love you." Then, he took his last long breathe and it was the end. I went back to my room and cried. My DoctorSon visited me in my room while I was crying and grieving. My DoctorSon is a medical doctor and suggested for me to live near him to oversee my situation. The next 2 days while Thomas was in the process of cremation, I was packing my clothes to stay at my son's house until I got my own apartment. Through these processes, I was just following commands from my son and Thomas's grown-up children from his previous marriage. I was not of myself.

After all the struggles I have been through from when Thomas started getting sick in year 2016 was seems a none ending at that moment. I could remember when he was going through of his Parkinson, and dementia I had to take care of him fully and there were many times Thomas would not follow doctor's advice. I felt worried until the end of his life that day. In my grieving period, I would gather his photos and hang them all over my walls in the cabana, and his ashes buried in my front yard near my meditation yoga area.

However, every time I passed by his burial in my yoga area, the remembrance of his life with me makes me grieve more. His ashes stay with indications of his burial, but it creates a very sad moment in me. My counselor had told me to remove his ashes and be buried in the cemetery. I plan to bring the ashes I saved in a small box to bring to my country where I was born. I plan to develop a cemetery for my family and bring his ashes to be buried with my family in this cemetery I plan to build.

Previously, I could not see and will not see Thomas' photos. I avoided it. Seeing Dr. Simpson helps me a lot to understand my situation, the suffering, grief, and the loss of my previous husband, Thomas. I was then able to see his photos in a slow process, but in the beginning only those happy photos, but not the sad and depressing ones. I then tried to be involved in church for activity. While in the beginning, my mind was somewhere else. The church goers see my physical being seems very devastated.

I was in the darkness of my life. Sometimes I do not hear them asking something. One of my sisterhoods in that church that my DoctorSon, and HisWife attend notices the sadness on my face due to grieving. Her name is Dottie. Dottie introduced herself to me and then we became friends. It didn't end there. I became a member of the church. This approach of my friend, Dottie helped me to have friends in the area where it was very new to me, thank you my dear friend Dottie, and her husband Reese. I then became part of the Prayer Team Group in the church.

After my previous husband (Thomas)passed away on

December 17, 2020, I moved from places to places giving me the unpleasant situation due to moving from place to another was not my interest. I felt like I was thrown out in the garbage can. But those moments of grieving I felt I was alone. Although my DoctorSon was helping me to grieve by referring me to Dr. Simpson as my counselor, the feeling of being alone in this walk of the river of life still existed within me at that time of grieving. However, in the long period of seeing a counselor, I somehow manage to handle my suffering of a complicated life situation. I was then able to see a counselor by myself. It helps me to see myself in the presence of reality of life if I just focus on myself and process my thoughts and understand the reality of the river of life. Although, I was in the moment living in bubbles, and I sometimes do not know myself then motivation to move forward slipped in within my thinking. Looking forward in a positive manner, I survived that to these days of my life I am still enjoying the new life I have with my new beginning.

Finally, I have now realized that the Lord has been speaking to me, but in the beginning, I had difficulty understanding. The question now is why am I still standing despites of struggles I went through? That's why I was able to be still standing because all along the Lord was with me through my struggles in life, holding me tightly not to fall. I am now listening and reading and understanding why am I still standing? The time has come, and I must get ready. "Follow me says the Lord" that sometimes I imagine that the angel is nearby to rescue me. I can imagine what was on my mind at that time I was like in prison feeling bonded to the situation at that moment, and every moment while in the process of realigning my life. Now I am awake and have realized that I was not alone at all. That's why I am still alive and exist in this world of chaos and plenty.

How to get out of this like imprisonment of my life is to listen to what the Lord was saying "follow me." I have realized that we as humans are letting ourselves magnetized for our own thinking from the past especially it created a big impact in your walk of life in this wide huge world of mixed beliefs of good and evil. Therefore, the title of my book that just got published in year 2021 is "The Two Universes of Self" I wrote this book because I want to see what's the inside of our mind that we have been keeping since when we were young and to these days of our lives while still living on this earth of plenty. Even Jesus was also tempted while he was praying. The same as we humans is to pray to be guarded by this type of thinking of imprisonment. Most of us don't think outside the box. Unaware that this thought we have in our mind can also be fulfilled by someone you've met. Filling in your needs through Words comes from your mind an example your mouth and may distract you or may satisfy you, such example of feeling lonely. Feeling "Lonely" can be one of those words to bring you to the world of loneliness. Also, these Words can be released from someone else mouth accidentally or intently if that someone understands and listens the heart and mind of that person. Sometimes it is accidental. The words we heard from our mouth or from someone else could be poisonous, and or helpful depending on what type of words coming out from your mouth and others. Are the WORDS comforting, or distracting?

In the beginning before hiring the builder who his name was also Thomas, which in this Memoir writing we call him "Tommy" to better understand of names similarities. We were introduced through the builder's stepfather, Richard, who was handling all the documentation and supposedly managing the workers in renovating our house. The other side of the story begins when I see my builder, Tommy and Thomas have similarities of many aspects as a man. Tommy looks like a young version of Thomas, my previous husband who died on December 17, 2020. I don't really believe in reincarnation, or astrological form of life in humans here on earth. Although just lately I found astrological form of life here on earth of humans seem like a cycle of life with each every one of us, such examples, Twin Flame, Soul Mates, which these words and meaning are very new to me.

To continue, on September 16, 2020, we got flooded and all things we have accumulated from 1950 to 2019 were thrown out in the five huge dumpsters I rented. The water was too high that the whole house must be fully repaired. I am sure that the situation was devastated by my previous husband while seeing the place we used to enjoyed together full of water, and all will be either abandoned or rebuilt. We must live in the hotel and move to motel for 2 months while looking for apartment or condo in the area to rent temporarily until the house that got flooded is fully renovated. The renovation process begins, and new life starts but common sense must be applied.

CHAPTER FIFTEEN

When Faith Determination Still Exist

The grieving, and loss of all my businesses I have developed, it is like the end, and it seems I must start the beginning of my life again. In addition to the grieving stage, I couldn't see myself moving forward and I felt like I was in the dark. I must enforce myself to open my mind to see the bright side. I would pray and pray. Through struggle due to grieving of Thomas' passing, I tried to accept the reality. Along with the grieving period I said to myself I must move forward. I would go into the process of digging into the past and into what had happened and how did I survive. The events were so fast such as remembering Covid ruined my businesses, sickness, flooding, sickness again, and death. I would cry and sob and scream louder and louder. Then, I went through silence, and just stared in one direction for an hour or two.

The feeling of hunger awakens me from silence and stare at nowhere moments. I did try to numb myself by drinking a tablespoon of red wine, but I ended up very drunk and slept for the whole day and night without waking up. Living by myself was a dangerous route of drinking a tablespoon of red wine which my body could not accept alcohol at all. I am not an alcohol drinker, and my immune system was not cooperating with my thought of numbness procedures, to forget the past. I had to go through these moments before I was able to see my life moving forward.

Covid, sickness, flood and more sickness and death devastated my life, and it seems that once we go into the other side of the fence that means to accept the reality, and look for ways on how to move forward, life starts over again in a positive manner. I felt stronger however, loneliness feeling was blocking my way to move forward. In addition to the processes of documents such as flood insurance process, and other insurances after all disastrous event in my life somehow numbness feeling of loneliness went away for a while, but only for a while. Then, it comes again once I am by myself. I kept thinking and convincing myself, such as dealing life, the real thing of what had happened such as covid, flood, sickness, and death I must prepare myself to face the reality.

To deal with flooding, I must interview many construction company workers to get quotes based on the rules of Allstate Insurance. I selected the 6th company I interviewed. While going back and forth at the house to check on the progress of the repair. I somehow meet this man who became my builder to renovate my house that got flooded. I see him when I visit the house, he, and his workers in the process of renovation. I look back and look back again, he looks so familiar. I stared at him and asked him if I knew him before. I asked him if he was one of my Bonifay Guild for the Arts (BGA) members. He said no. I asked him if he had been to Houston Texas. He said yes. I asked him if he had a yellow sports car, a thunderbird. He said he had a yellow triumph motorcycle. He showed me the photo of his yellow motorcycle. I would stare at him and in my mind, he looked like my husband in his younger years of 20s to 40s. I could not forget the photos of Thomas' younger years. I somehow connect the images of the photos in my mind and watching this man who repaired my house.

There were times I tried to walk away just to clear my mind. And I would ask the questions within me talking to myself and realizing to question myself such as am I in cloud nine? There are times I somehow ignore the images in my mind. Trying to convince myself that I am still in the period of grieving. I am seeing Thomas, my previous husband younger years through this man, the builder named Tommy. I also found out that his first name is the same as my previous husband, Thomas. His nickname is also the same as Tommy. However, to avoid confusion in this book of "The Memoir: The River Of Life" let us call my builder, Tommy, and my previous husband, Thomas, not to get confused as I already mentioned above.

Because of my curiosity I decided to talk more about these issues of similarities. I must talk to this man again, my builder named Tommy. I stopped by my house that they are renovating to see him, and I could not stop asking questions again. I asked him how many children he has. What does he do if he is not renovating houses. Just for curiosity as if is he really a good builder. He was in the air force and as a pilot. He was telling me about his daughter of

7 and his son of 9 years old. He is somehow passionate about his children which really brings me back to my volunteering years with Guardian Ad Litem which just recently I am now back of being a GALP volunteer to protect the abused and neglected children in the USA. I visit families and children neglected by their parents. Also, I am the voice of neglected and abused children in three counties where I have been living for more than 20 years.

I see this man as a caring and loving father to his children which really puts my heart into more visualization of who he is. I admire him for being compassionate to his children. I feel like my emptiness filled in while talking to this man. We started texting and through texting I enjoy communicating with him. Somehow my feeling of loneliness became joyful and filled. More questions I asked, and he sounds like me. Our interests and work habits are similar. We even joking in our text about maybe buying a truck like his. In our texting messages I was alive laughing with icons of LOL throughout the text. I became attached, attracted, and addicted to him. I constantly text him just to have fun, and laughter. I became alive.

Although I still have the grieving of my previous husband, Thomas' passing, my emptiness deep within me filled with laughter with my builder, Tommy. With prayers to the Lord to fill in my life of meaningful remembrance of life here on earth, this man, who gave me the beginning of my life again with lots of joy and laughter that I have been dreaming of instead of crying due to grieving the death of my previous husband, Thomas. I felt and I would like to say this "I intently and chose to move forward." However, common sense, and protecting my reputation, then that's the beginning of the end.

CHAPTER SIXTEEN

Loneliness Versus Aloneness: Temptation Begins

In the Bible says, that Temptation is not a sin. *"In the day when I called, you answered me; and You strengthen me with strength (might and inflexibility to temptation) in my inner self (Psalm 138:3). Temptation to do wrong can make you feel horrible. You may think I shouldn't be going through this; I shouldn't be having a problem with this. But God taught me that temptation isn't sin;* **we sin when we give in to temptation. The Bible says temptation will come**. *It doesn't say, "Woe unto him to whom it comes," it says, "Woe unto him by whose hand it comes" (see Matthew 17:7).* Jesus told us to pray that we **would not give in to the temptation when we are tempted** (see Luke 22:40). Psalm 105:4 is a great way to start your day right, it says, *"Seek, inquire of and for the Lord, and crave Him and His strength (His might and inflexibility to temptation); seek and require His face and His presence (continually) evermore."* (Meyer, p.294).

Loneliness begins when I was living by myself, then temptation follows. Rebuilding my house that got flooded is like rebuilding my life for renewing life activity. When Thomas, my previous husband passed away in December 2020 that was until my counselor advised me to let it go. Although, waking up and heading through the tunnel of darkness, it seems like I am moving forward to a new life to hope to see the light at the end of a tunnel. However, my knowledge of repairing the house was like in kindergarten. I have no idea what I need to do. I do believe in prayer and a saying that we break down first then getting up for all things will be new again. I do not know how to begin but suddenly, the closeness of our friendship that instead of client business relationship but more into an attraction within developed along the way through texting and seeing each other.

This relationship created havoc between a client and contractor's life. However, since both him and I have good self-control we only had business development instead, we created such a business such as a limousine business and motorcycling together. Through seeing each other with self-control we had develop a plan to go motorcycling for fun and suddenly motorcycle was bought by me but due to built-in self-control of mine as only for business relationship plus finding out that he was married everything changed in a heartbeat. Although we had developed a friendly relationship with built self-control not to get into more than just friends, we were successful, however. Likewise, within us there were some interests but at least I felt it. It seems like my emptiness was filled in and complete but still grieving of my late husband's passing. While writing this passage I can't help to cry. I cried because I felt like at that time of my grieving and emptiness of being alone there was someone who I am texting to comfort me in my grieving stage with his encouraging words and positivity in life while I was in the brink of breaking down. I am thankful to the Lord. Encourage me to be strong and I can move forward. Through prayers, I was thankful to the Lord that I found this man on this earth of plenty at the time of suffering due to grieving. However, feeling of intimacy developed more than just close friends that somehow, I must reveal for me to be aware that I am his client, and he is my builder. As both of us have our self-control in order this feeling of mine and his must be revealed for us to be alerted and be cautious.

Therefore, there it was that I told him about my feeling and how I feel that we need to be separated and we must stop this closeness as friends, too close that this feeling of ours could develop an intimate relationship. However, on his side and I will never forget this word he spoke, *"If you have a feeling for me and you will distance yourself then it will become a problem."* And it became a problem yes, it is and was that breaks his heart and mine. Therefore, I said to myself that the benefit of this was I caution myself and avoid complication of the situation mixing business versus personal feeling. Then the separation between the two of us became so confusing and must use what I learned from my major in PhDs, in mixing business versus personal feelings.

Then the separation between the two of us became very hurtful and confusing. We struggle to be involved in any issue in renovation of my house which is unavoidable. Our division from each other created a mess that it went through so many hurts and distractions in finishing my house for renovation, the limousine business and the motorcycling for fun must be stopped and discontinued. All personal activities between me and him such as texting, eating out, and many more must be stopped.

However, connectivity between me and Tommy continues, but it is in a very different manner of connectivity. Somehow, there was a bruise of this type of connectivity. Although, on his part, he seemed very open and now active in being fully connected, and I am hearing the words "I love you, Sofia" from him, which I thought we had already been disconnected from personal activities. After disconnecting from our personal activities together, he was very agitated. He then created a scene that I was not expecting, such as bringing a woman to the church where I go. This woman had a child, and he is intently trying to make me jealous. I know that he knew that I was going to that church because I told him before this chaos happened between me and him. The woman he brought to this church used to be a member of the church I went to. She quit being a member for so long, and then that day, she came over with him. It was difficult to understand the ins and outs of Tommy's behavior, and therefore, I must decide to cut it off fully. However, he was telling me that he and his wife would get divorced. That was his plan before he met me, he said. Again, I do believe that the Lord knows my suffering and needs, and not needs within my life. I always follow what the Lord is telling me through Good Common Sense, Wisdom, and Conscience.

CHAPTER SEVENTEEN

Self-Controlled: Faith Being Tested

Since that I was trying not get involved with any man and if I am I need to heal myself first. I chose to be by myself. Also, I am making sure that a man I must be with is not married. I do not want to ruin marriages of someone's life. As I have experienced when I met BreadWinnerMan who is the father of my EldestSon in year 1970s, I was a mistress. However, there is a possibility that I may go back to that due to many temptations I have encountered. Therefore, I must apply Self-Control.

My builder, Tommy is a very kind a person, respectful and seems I was comforted by him at that time of my grieving stage. After finding out that he was married, but supposedly to divorce his wife, everything changed. Therefore, a self-control attitude must be applied in this type of situation. I watch out for my action towards having a relationship with my builder, Tommy, despite loneliness and similarities between my previous husband Thomas, and my builder, Tommy.

We as humans, there are always many types of temptations in life. Are these temptations being confusing such as type of feeling within our hearts and mind, the similarities, the comforts, and many other feelings we have within us that we feel protected and felt loved by someone specially you are alone, temptation begins in so many ways. I decided to go in the other direction instead of what he had already said that it would become a problem in avoiding my feelings for him. Although, I feel kind of love at first sight, but I watched out myself and handled the humanly loneliness and the uncomforted feelings while still grieving with my previous husband's passing.

I told my builder, Tommy, to wait until my house was sold to pay him for the remaining balance of $25,000. However, this issue became so chaotic between me and him. Tommy's response to my decision to avoid him due to our feeling of intimacy connection was developing. He answered me in a sarcastic tone. This is his email to me while I was in the process of departing from him to disconnect our feeling of intimacy from each other.

"Seriously?? Because I cannot wait for the house to be sold. I have made myself very, very, very clear on this. Waiting is not an option. It has never been an option. You have had months and months to prepare your house to be completed. There is not one single contractor that works pro bono or spends thousands of dollars. I spent tens of thousands of dollars on a project just to wait to be compensated. I simply do not understand what is so difficult about you understanding this. Having faith in the Lord has absolutely nothing to do with a contract; instead of wasting your time and energy on looking for future projects and condos, you need to be working on getting me paid. I will not wait. The first two episodes of this were the

loss draft department's faults. This is all you (Carr, 2021)."

Every morning I usually pray. That special morning, I prayed and thankful to the Lord about meeting this man in my life. I have noticed that I was singing in the morning and being joyful all day long. However, I must emphasize the difference between Self-Expression and Action. Self- Expression is to release what's in the mind to communicate what's stored in the mind. To act of these thoughts understanding may differ for each event, and for each one of us. Releasing the contents of the mind eases up the burden of too many kept memories or to be caution and alerted is through conversation with someone, or release what's in my mind that gives me the burden, shall I call this burden, the cargo? There are ways on how to do it just like in a pleasant way, and or professional way to avoid complication. However, my builder, Tommy, misunderstood all that I said. Also, his ego was touched, and I've hurt his feeling as a man. But one day he wants me to visit the renovation process. I came to the place, but he showed me his divorce papers, in proving that he is now divorced. But my decision to re-connect with him is over due to his behavior I didn't like after all.

Perhaps, through frustrations Tommy was upset due to many unpleasant events circumstances, such example, my decision to pull away from him. Our personal business together that has been developed such as the limousine business, the motorcycling activity must be stopped that includes the checking account for the business. However, the connectivity between me and him continues due to my house is still in the process of renovation, but carefully not to be connected in a personal way where feelings of both of us develop again.

To be intact for self-control as a widow, I would say I've been tested with feelings and temptations many times. Being a widow and living alone, I developed a lonely feeling of aloneness. Feeling empty and lonely is not a good place for a widow who has and recognizes the practice of boundaries and self-control. Thus, being alone, the strategy is to meet people. I ended up meeting many men in my life instead. My mind is thinking that I must meet people for me to survive here on earth, friends, that is. However, it is to the extreme that I somehow cut it down to the limit for me to control and build boundaries so temptation will be blocked.

Although, it was not my intention to just meet any man but anyone that I could have conversation of my experience as a widow. I was also trying to find all my friends, members and BGA volunteers I had when I had my businesses. Due to covid, and flooding, I found out that the people I knew moved to another locations, states and cities. However, it just happened that men are more active to become and request as my friends especially in Facebook form of invitation. Invitations multiply through texting from Facebook and different locations which I was not aware of. This form is away from physical temptation however between a man and a woman kind of a type of activity. For example, I made a selfie of myself in the form of a mean face but every comment I received says it is beautiful and not a" mean face" at all. I was puzzled. In the beginning without explanatory reasonings I was very confused. I did send that face to Facebook to discourage men to friend request, but it's the opposite happened such as more than ten men sent message of friend request instead.

I then removed my mean photo to change a natural face that is. Also, I was so surprised that I can be friends with people outside USA countries. However, the reason to friend request by these men has many different reasons and most I do not accept due to my boundary and self-control that given me the time to analyze who these men are and what are the reasons to be friended in Facebook. I finally solved the puzzle. I have my son help me to remove and delete all friend requests on FB. That solved the issues of looking for friends on FB.

Therefore, I was scared for a while, so I promised myself not to participate in any activity through FB. Again, my son was guiding me and told me to avoid those men sending friend requests on FB. I followed my son's advice. I then started again to be alone. Being alone, I went back to hiding in my cave, my cabana. I then calmed down and separated myself from too many friend requests of men on FB. Because of these types of activity on FB, I totally avoided them all. That solved the issues from the friend request activity on

FB. I think. Well, not really. Every time I go grocery shopping at Walmart or whatever department store I go to, I somehow feel like someone is following me. I would pinch myself just to see if I am just imagining due to my experiences since when I was young and to these days. I found out that when we imagine and form an illusion of what we are thinking, it becomes real. I asked myself what the heck was going on! I then start to pray deep within me.

I chose to live in a newly renovated barn I called Cabana. The Cabana is in a very secluded location. I am on the boondock side of living situation in a gated 3-acre land. The gate is always locked day and night. Living by myself has given me the isolation phenomena that I have never experienced before. However, for me to make meaning to my living situation, I made these 3 acres of land with Cabana as my late husband Thomas' sanctuary. I designed it and planted some flowers. I encountered many wild animals coming to the Sanctuary. There are wild, beautiful flowers growing, and green grass is well-cut by my gardeners. I have many deer passing by looking for food. I decided to buy corn for their meal and, at the same time, enjoy seeing them while they are eating corn on the ground. I enjoy the deer in my front yard, and I hear birds singing. I started becoming a hermit.

I have gardeners and workers to take care of my surroundings while enjoying wild animals living in the area. In the morning, when the sun starts to rise, I would do my meditation. My gardener and carpenters made a meditation area in the middle of the 3 acres of land surrounded by many trees, green grass, and birds singing. Wisteria flowers are blooming, and vines are crawling up top of the roof of my yoga or meditation area. It was a calming and peaceful surrounding I had created with the help of my workers. These peaceful surroundings were very enjoyable to be surrounded by it. However, I must get my groceries for my food and needs while living in the boondocks, a gated and very secluded place with many trees and wild animals passing through. I encountered people who I did not know. I was a little bit of a person that scared of people when I met them due to my experiences being alone in the Cabana for a while. My first grocery shopping was to gather canned foods and to preserve food type of living. I filled up 2 shelves with everything type of canned foods and bags of rice. The only time I had to get groceries was to have fresh vegetables if my vegetable garden ran out of them.

Before Thomas, my previous husband, passed away, I encountered this type of incident, whatever you call it. It happened when he was still alive. However, I felt protected at that time when he was with me going to Walmart or wherever we went. When someone approached me to be a friend, and this person was a man, Thomas was with me all the time. He would block this man who approached me, and I felt safe. If some guy would stare at me and ask my name, Thomas, my previous husband, would block that person, and I would feel protected somehow. I then prepared myself to dress like a professional and speak like an intelligent woman. But it didn't work, and still, I get attention due to the fact that I am a small-stature woman and act like a child.

I then changed how I dressed and made myself like an ordinary individual to avoid attention. However, I didn't feel comfortable with what I was wearing, such as loose garments or slippers or something to look like a sloppy individual. As a PhDs individual, I also tried to dress like I was a professional, but that didn't work either. I then decided that I would be and am who I am. I then feel comfortable, and I do not have to be afraid or fear about what happened next.

However, these new events in my life, being alone and being by myself, are new to me, and I do not know how to handle this issue in the beginning. I could remember my childhood experiences, and I felt that it was coming back again, or was this just my imagination or hallucination? I must examine myself through my new activities. After Thomas' passing, I was very cautious about living by myself. I see myself as again becoming a victim of men. This self-reflection as being alone after Thomas' passing on December 17, 2020, all one seems I am again becoming the prey of vultures in the wild.

With these experiences in life, I became stronger than ever before. Being a selective woman with whom I will be a married couple helps me to choose the right man in my life. In my selection process, I made sure that I am not and will not merge myself with the wild world. Choosing the right way and making the right decision is very important to me. I always use the skills the Lord has given us, all humans here on earth. These are Good Common Sense, Good Wisdom, and Good Conscience that we must use while on our temporary journey here on earth of plenty. I am shielded with God's grace and blessings to be able to distinguish between right and wrong, peace and chaos.

CHAPTER EIGHTEEN

Motivational Word That Kept Me Alive

I do believe that God is always working for our needs in life. He always gives us someone to be with for us to share our experiences in life with others we encounter in this temporary journey on earth and for someone to consult when in life disarray. However, always follow the Lord's intention. The intention is that sometimes, as human beings, we misunderstand. We need to understand that there are two types of relationships and feelings to distinguish between our earthly being and the spiritual world. The agape love to all brothers and sisters and the intimate love between a man and a woman as a married couple are the two meanings of love. We, as humans, already have those two kinds of love. A man and a woman in a relationship as a married couple have the license to have sexual intimacy for the sake of reputable distinction as a solid togetherness as a married couple with God's grace. This type of solid togetherness as a married couple with God's grace has changed these days. It is difficult to distinguish between the two. However, using God's instinctive talent, such as good common sense, good wisdom, and good conscience, you will be safe in your journey on earth with a mix of good and evil types of activity.

One day, I was too fast in planning and developing a limousine business regarding what we needed to do, such as opening a business account. Previously, five days before, Tommy, my business partner, told me to "SLOW DOWN." Either coincidental or meant to be the same day, April 8th, 2021, as I always open my prayer book and devotional book I read every morning, and the word "Slow Down" repeated which the title of the prayer book I read is "SLOW DOWN." I cried. I cried because of the two words that were important to me when Tommy, my business partner, told me to slow down. I have always been a person who is always in the Fast Phase Lane of life, making decisions to rush into things that sometimes go to disastrous results.

I cried because it seemed someone was always with me to look after me seemed I was in a safe zone of life. However, staying away from my builder, Tommy, due to my decision for us to break this type of feeling of ours, I felt like I was alone again. Although being alone again, I felt relief on the other side of me due to the feeling of self-control brought me to the other side of decision-making and learning from my mistakes. I may ask if this event in my life is coincidental or whatever you called it because my previous husband Thomas and my builder have many similarities. Although Tommy, my builder, is younger than my previous husband Thomas, seeing and feeling the similarities somehow cures my aloneness at that time of my grieving Thomas' passing. Such as many examples is the word always. Thomas, my previous husband, would say to me, *"Slow Down."* When Tommy, my builder, would also say the word "Slow Down," it brings memories from my previous life with Thomas and, of course, my previous builder Tommy the two words, "SLOW DOWN," such meaningful words I could not forget.

Again, I could also remember my sister Annie saying these two words, "Slow Down," while we were walking in the mountains on Bohol Island, heading to *Kawasan, the Waterfall of Bohol Island.* The two words I will never forget. When I decide too fast on things to be done, it will be done, but sometimes it goes in a different direction, and I didn't expect it. My previous husband, Thomas, my builder, Tommy, and my sister, Annie, would say the same two words, "Slow Down." Then, just recently, my husband Cameron would say, "Slow Down." Amazing! I would say listen to your surroundings, and it gives you a hint on if you are doing right or wrong. It somehow guided you to where it was supposed to be.

The lesson to learn is that somehow, there are angels around us we didn't even know. Angel form within someone whom the Lord entrusted here on earth with us in every human being living here on earth. Then, someone would express it, and we are surprised we hear it again from someone. That it had been stated the word "Slow Down" in my experience that I needed at that moment within us in the spiritual world.

Hearing the words repeatedly has given me the thinking of I better slow down and think first before acting. My emotions and feelings were acknowledged. We all have emotions and feelings, and I have been using mine all the way. Having friends and remembering the words settled in my mind, walking through the darkness in life, I somehow overcame.

I do believe that the Lord wants me to be still and have peace despite of so much chaos in my life such as Covid 19 I lost my businesses, flooding devastated and lost all our things on earth of plenty, sickness, and death, but I am still surviving somehow. I called this incident as it meant to be for me that the Lord wants me to still exist on this earth of plenty.

Once again, running away with a heavy load, I was unable to get away from darkness. I was unable to run away with a heavy load carrying with me. I tried to pray but only to get upset about why I was on this road of loneliness and aloneness, and the path to go through was so dark I could not see where I was heading. I cried and screamed, but again, no one heard me. I started reading my Bible. This is what I found in *Matthew 6:25-34 Jesus said not to be anxious about anything, for God knows your needs and promises to care for you.* I kept that in mind.

I focused myself in reading my Bible and I kept going. Somehow, reading my Bible I find some answers that comforted me, and I somehow without knowing have then managed to keep going. The feeling of someone is with me at the time of prayer was very interesting because the feeling of aloneness somehow partly disappeared. I said partly because in my Thought Universe, I still must convince the Physic Universe that it's okay to be alone. The struggles I have encountered between the Thought Universe and the Physic Universe to merge and help one another through feeling, thinking, and acting what's inside my Thought Universe was difficult in the beginning. Therefore, I continue my habit of prayer to these days.

CHAPTER NINETEEN

The Lord's Master Plan Becomes Visible

When I was growing up with 6 sisters all together, my parents always giving us a warning like this, "no *sexual activity before marriage.*" I can remember I was outside with a friend, a friend boy that holding hands together and I was only 15 years old. My sister notified my mother about this boy, and I was holding hands together. My mother called me with an angry voice saying, "Child come inside the house now, now!" I was so frightened, and I asked myself "What did I do? My mom explained to me "No Sex Before Marriage." And I said we were just holding hands. My mom says, that's the start then it goes to a different direction. My sisters laughed at me like I did something wrong.

These warning signs and or shall I say lesson I've learned from our parents with 6 daughters now became ladies, still vivid in my mind. Therefore, I always think, and used my common sense and conscience between a man and woman relationship. But of course, I was defiant therefore my relationship with BreadWinnerMan was hidden secret for long. My conscience and common sense kept bugging me to reopen and come to light. So, I left my privilege of living and went in a different direction. However, this defiant behavior although it exists at the time of my youth the journey here on earth, the lesson I learned from my parents still within my spiritual world that kept me to a safe direction when it comes to temptation in life then and now being a widow at age 64.

Being alone, however, as a widow has given me the sense of learning myself through listening to the birds singing and watching deer, and many other wild animals in the woods. I then started painting them on canvas. I reopened my art classes business but it's more of an exclusive and my students would do plein air painting, painting directly from what we see, like wild animals and birds flying. It was fun. However, the memory from the past still lingered in my mind when I'm alone. Every morning when I wake up my heart is feeling squeezed due to remembrance of those moments.

In similarity, my friend Jasmin met a man when her husband passed away in January 2020. Jasmin and her husband used to be my tenants. Then everything changed when COVID came, and I must sell my apartment units in Bonifay downtown. So, for how many years, I have had no communications with my organization's members, volunteers, tenants, art students, and Jasmin as one of my previous tenants.

One day, I was at Walmart for groceries and Jasmin called my name. Then we talked about life on what's going on and she said that her husband passed away in January 2020. My previous husband Thomas, passed away in December 2020. Such a coincidence when someone is very similar to my situation, we re-connected. I then have someone to talk about the grieving period, and many other incidents and accidents happened when Covid, hurricane, sickness and death came to our lives. Jasmin became my art student.

So, Jasmin and I talked about the past. I told her that I sold my rental properties to a retired police officer from Miami who saw my advertisement, and therefore I have been disconnected with all my friends and businesses when also Covid came. I lost all my business and I only focused on my husband's health. I went through the tunnel of the darkest event in my life. The grieving period puts me in bad health, and I lost too much weight that I must keep up with my doctor.

Just lately, in February 2022 I was living in my big new house just finished renovation and it was for sale, and it got sold in March 2022. Now I am back but in a different way. The renovation of my house that got flooded on September 16, 2020, by Sally Hurricane also puts me into another darkest tunnel in my life. With all my burdens and struggles, I asked myself how did I survive? Somehow, I did it anyway. I always play the song "There Was Jesus" that makes me keep going with hope, faith and determination that is.

To these days, I always listen to Christian songs with

guidance and eye-opening type of songs. It also helps me to keep in line. I always remember that "Words" is powerful. We hear it and it goes directly within our mind. It creates a place within our Thought Universe. Then, it becomes alive if we believe in it. Therefore, the Physic Universe acts on it to be seen to the world. Surprisingly, I have survived the many devastating life events in my life. The Lord's masterplan continues in a different way which we as humans do not understand. At this time of my grieving, God's master plan started to become visible through putting pieces together of incidents and accidents. Living at my cabana by myself was a totally different type of lifestyle to what I had never been, I said to Jasmin. She also told me about how she suffered when her husband passed away. Jasmin's story will be in another book I am putting it together title "Hey!"

Being in prayer every morning gives me guidance in life instructions on how and when to proceed. I have read Joyce Meyer devotional reading and prayer. I then developed a group called "Prayer Is Powerful" group. This started with only 5 members and now has more than 300 members from all over the world. I share these readings and prayers to my members of *"Sofia's Prayer Is Powerful."* This group continues to these days.

To continue Jasmin and our conversation, after the renovation of my main house, instead of 8 bedrooms, it cuts off to a 4-bedroom house and 2 baths. Because selling an 8-bedroom house could be so strange and unfamiliar to some, the reason that the house had 8 bedrooms was because I rented the 4 bedrooms to earn income while taking care of my previous husband, Thomas, while he was in the process of having Parkinson's and dementia. I can't relax myself to not to work. When my previous husband started to get sick, I dropped all that I was doing, such as closing all my businesses due to COVID-19, sickness and flooding in the area. Then, the flooding in 2020 did cause more devastation to our lives. Everything changed, including my life routine of being a businesswoman.

In March 2022, the main house with 4 bedrooms and 2 baths was sold on 9 acres land. Then, the proceed sale of the house I paid off all bills such as hospitals and emergency bills, including my RAV4 2021 and renovation of the barn now I called it the *Cabana*. Living in the Cabana after renovation with of course walls color outside and inside, and doors color in and out I love it. I chose gray walls and red for all doors. I enjoyed living in my Cabana with beautiful views and so secluded because I have my workers fenced off the whole area of 3 acres of land, higher private fence that is.

In continuing my conversation with Jasmin, I also told her about how I managed my life. It was a relief to have someone to talk to, a friend with similar situation because her husband died, and she also suffered. However, on the other side of my life I felt something was missing. Therefore, there are so many temptations that come to life. I also went and continue going to my counselor due to grieving.

I can't focus to move forward due to crying every 2 o'clock in the morning waking up and sobbing.

Also, the feeling of something is missing in my life, and it seems it doesn't make sense at all. Jasmin and I story has a similarity. Jasmin has a son, 6 years old at that time. Jasmin talked about her boyfriend, named Nelson. We then begin comparing who they were. At that time, he was with Nelson. But there are issues. At that time Tommy, my builder, also had an issue with me. Nelson and Tommy have a similar attitude. Is this a coincidence? The story about Jasmin and Nelson will be in my book title "Hey!" But this incident was helping me to cope with my grieving talking to someone, a friend who I knew previously as my tenant and an art student, a similarity of the story gives me going to talk about because there are connectivity's of the past. The Lord always gives us a friend to talk to and somehow similar incident as what I have encountered. Amazing! The similarity of our experiences between men who we have encountered, we then have something to talk about. We then laugh out loud, and somehow, we enjoyed that moments while doing art painting on canvas.

To continue, my children already have their own lives. My older son has four boys, and my younger son has 2 children. In my cabana, however, I am accompanied by wild natural resources such as birds and wild animals. And with my art classes on going such art painting on canvas with my students it was more productive and creative. Therefore, I then again taught art classes to the few art students I have had that includes Jasmin.

I continued telling Jasmin that before living full time in my Cabana, I used to live in Tallahassee near my DoctorSon. But I was renting an apartment which cost me more than $1,100 a month plus electricity, and water. It was not wise at all for me to rent an apartment that I already have my own house. I called it the "Cabana" it's free and clear, that means no mortgage payment. So, I insisted on moving back from nearby my DoctorSon house to my Cabana which is an hour and a half drive from Tallahassee.

My DoctorSon and I always have a disagreement about me living by myself in a secluded place where I do not know anyone at that time. Although the cabana is just behind my main house that got sold, since it's all fenced in and in a very secluded place, it looked like I was isolated from anyone. I understand my son's worries and concerns. I do appreciate my dear DoctorSon, who is now a medical doctor.

Being alone, which I was alone anyway at my apartment when I was living in Tallahassee, I should be able to handle being alone in my own Cabana, I thought. I do not need to pay the rent of the apartment near my son. The Cabana is paid in full and no mortgage payment at all. That's the winner, no mortgage payment. Well, by the way I was a mortgage closer/signing agent previously before disasters came to my life. I know what I am paying regarding mortgage payments. I say bye, bye to that. I am free of monthly payments of mortgage, insurances, and many more. This story will be in my next book titled "Feudalistic Era In 21st Century."

Anyhow, to continue living by myself in my new renovated Cabana, I felt alone that every time I passed by my neighborhood, I do not know who my neighbors are. All I know are the people who bought our main house with 4 bedrooms with 9 acres land, and our long-time neighbor, Gail. Passing through my new address where my new renovated Cabana is on a 3 acre of land, I somehow see this house on left coming from my gate to the main road. The name of the road where my Cabana is located is Will Lee Road. I pass this house on the left I passed by every time I go to town, and or in Dothan at Barnes and Noble or to go shopping at Kohls or watch movie, I always pass this house on the left heading out the main road, and or on the right heading back to my Cabana. I always have a beginning and end episodes of my life journey here on earth of plenty. Meeting my neighbors in the area where my cabana is located is another episode of life journey and its beginning.

CHAPTER TWENTY

The 1695: Meeting My Neighbor

Previously, I never really knew my neighbors in the area because we were all busy working in life. Now that I am living by myself, businesses were closed, and my previous husband passed away, I was also planning to reopen my businesses to become a busy person again in my time of being alone. But these plans I must reopen my business were sort of my goals to be fulfilled, but it did not happen.

These incidents were from 2006 to 2021. Not every day that I received mails that were not ours but most of the week. Sometimes I would bring these mails to the post office and complain. I explained to the Post Office manager that 1695 Will Lee Road and 1695 Hwy 177 are totally different mailboxes. The Post Office personnel asked for forgiveness. But it didn't stop there. It keeps going and delivering mail from the same address. This time I ignored it and just put a note that it is not mine, and "Return To Sender" words in big letters. In January 2022 coming back to Panhandle Florida from Tallahassee living near my DoctorSon, after disastrous events in my life, everything is very new to me.

However, let me begin explaining the very puzzles of my life that I didn't understand in the beginning. That until to this day I could not believe that it was happening, and here I am still alive and living a good life, I would say. As mentioned, by the time the main house was renovated and sold in March 2022, I renovated the barn now I called a cabana that I used to use as my art studio before the flood. This barn became my home from Tallahassee moved back to Panhandle Florida and I live in my now Cabana on 3 acres land with beautiful views and fenced all around the house and the entrance is with a lock gated property. I have gathered my workers to renovate the barn and continue the cleaning of my surroundings which before it was my walking trail, and meditation area.

Now with the new renovated cabana with meditation area plus clean walking trail, I truly enjoyed my walk here on earth of plenty. I was able to listen to birds singing early in the morning. It is a calm and quite place to live in. However, I feel like I am by myself, and the aloneness feeling, and lonely feeling comes to my mind and heart. I then tried to know my neighbors around which they were my previous neighbors, but we never see or maybe we've seen our previous neighbors, but we don't' pay attention due to busy working, or things that we do every day.

After renovation of my Cabana, I am very curious who are my neighbors. Although, my previous husband Thomas and I have lived in this area since the year 2004, but on the other side of my previous property which I only knew is Gail my close neighbor of the main house that I sold in March 2022. Every time I passed by in this house which is across from my cabana with so many trees that covers the house address 1695 Will Lee Road, I try to know who lives across my property.

I met some of the residents in the area in a quiet neighborhood of Will Lee Road in the small town of Panhandle, Florida. Every time I see people on the road from the main highway to Will Lee Road and getting out of my agricultural style gate, I feel I am not alone living by myself when I see people on the road where my Cabana is located. This place was away from hustle and bustle in a very secluded place. I used to live in a city with lots of people, but after the disastrous life I have been through, I changed my living style. I would remember my dear DoctorSon commented to me on how I would be able to live in the "boondock" kind of living style, alone and no one there to help me if I needed help. However, my place, the cabana I called it, is so peaceful and tranquil. I love it. Again, I, however, am interested in getting to know the people in my new location.

One day, I saw a Van parking on the other side of my property across the road, I would say across my property but there are so many trees in between that I could not see better who lives there across my property. When I pass by this house, I always see a van and a white car parked but that day I passed by this house, the van somehow, I didn't see in the parking lot of this house. I was puzzled. Was someone stealing the van? I questioned myself. So many questions in my mind that passing by every time I go to Barnes and Nobles for my book writing and editing. My mind was busy thinking who lives there across my property. My cabana is covered with lots of trees, and my gate is always locked. I was reluctant to introduce myself because I do not know what I would encounter if I approached them first. This time, I am always careful of my actions.

I decided to get to know my neighbors and I met Heather who had three children in the neighborhood. She would go to the road to take her children to the bus stop for school. Then, I met other neighbors with children. However, the house with the van and a white car, I have never met this person or this family yet. Maybe they have children also. Before Covid and hurricane, I used to be with Guardian Ad Litem as a volunteer visiting neglected and abused children in 3 counties. I was just wondering if this neighbor of mine across my gated Cabana also has children.

I was about to open my gate to get in. I saw a man in the mailbox. I stared at him, and he also stared at me but very quickly and he left. I never see children with him or a wife. I said to myself, maybe this man is also a hermit does not want to meet people like me. So, every time I passed by the house there was always a question in my mind such as wondering who lives at this address 1695 Will Lee Road. I do remember before Covid, hurricane, and death, I always received letter from this address which is the same address number of the house 1695, but different road name.

I am now trying to know who my new neighbors are on the other side of my property. I am willing to know my neighbors around my 3 acres land with cabana and is gated. The curiosity of who my neighbor in 1695 address was bringing back to when there were many mails, I received from the Post Man due to mistaken address, 1695 Hwy 177 and 1695 Will Lee Road. I decided to solve the puzzles I have had in my mind since then as to why these mails of 1695 Will Lee Road were always in my mailbox 1695 Hwy 177. I am now trying to solve the mysterious incident of exchanging mails of the unknown residence from the year 2006 to 2022.

I was curious who lives there at 1695 Will Lee Road address. It could be too complicated but let me explain for clarification because it is very confusing. The main house I sold after renovation in March 2022 is also 1695 number but in a Hwy 177. The place where my Cabana is located is a very quiet neighborhood which is at 1680 Will Lee Road. There are not many cars passing by in this area. It is a secluded little town and very quiet neighborhood. I tried to know the neighbors by sightseeing who passes by the area.

Although, my entrance is too complicated because you drive into the gate, and you must follow the lights on the ground where the entrance is. I intently made this type of living with a lock gate, a long turn around entrance of the driveway, lights all over the ground for guidance to the Cabana, and yoga area, lights on the ground for safety driving at night in the middle of the woods, and security cameras are all over the property. I can see who is going in and out my property, even the wild animals I can see them through my cell phone.

Again, passing through this road every day heading to Dothan or downtown is always a puzzle to me who lives at 1695 Will Lee Road address. In my mind, I could remember in my mailbox while living in our main house 1695 Hwy 177 I always received mails in that the name of "Cameron address 1695 Will Lee Road." I would make a note to a mail delivery person that this name "Cameron" does not live at 1695 Hwy 177. Sometimes, I have made a note to mail delivery person that says, "read before dropping it in my mailbox, okay?"

Since April 2022 I now living full time in my new renovated Cabana after selling my main house in March of 2022, I now seeing this address 1695 Will Lee Road now that my new address is 1680 Will Lee Road. My memory of this address confuses me in the beginning of thinking and putting incidents together to understand what had happened. Puzzles came to my thoughts, and I was trying to solve it. Every time I pass by this address 1695 Will Lee Road; the puzzle begins to throttle my memories. Since year 2004 to 2021 I do not know all my neighbors while living in 1695 Hwy 177 because I concentrate and focused on my businesses such as mortgage closing and signing, Notary Public service, Art Gallery and Art Studio, and rental properties.

Covid came and these businesses were blocked and closed. I can only continue my arts and book writing because I do not need to be with people, and I do it myself in my Cabana or wherever I am. The busyness in life can be a blockage of knowing who your neighbors are, and people nearby.

Passing by again every day in this house, my mind kept thinking who lives at this address of 1695 Will Lee Road. I have counted many times of every moment I am interested in introducing myself who lives in this address 1695 Will Lee Road. I am looking forward to meeting my neighbors now that I have time to get to know them all.

One day, going to my new road where my cabana was situated, passing through 1695 Will Lee Road heading to Barnes and Noble to continue my book writing, I always see on the left-hand side a house, but I cannot see who is in that house. I only see the Van, and a white car. The next day I passed by I saw only the white car. I counted how many days the van was not in the driveway. It was 3 days that the van was gone, but the white car was still there. The next 8 days I passed by again to head to Publix for groceries and I saw the van in the driveway, but the white car was gone. I was just curious who lives at 1695 Will Lee Road due my experiences previously in year 2006 through 2020 the mail delivery always made mistakes of putting mails at my address mailbox 1695 Hwy 177.

Not to get confused, let me explain how these similarities got so intense that I must solve the mysterious connection between me and my neighbor at 1695 Will Lee Road. How I met my neighbor Cameron in year 2022 was such a puzzle to me until these days. My neighbor Cameron and I talked about it about his mails kept getting into my mailbox. Putting these puzzles together we found out that there was a connection to knowing each other.

God's plan sometimes we do not understand and in that moment, we do not know where to go. To follow God's plan is so smooth and no struggles at all. We called it "it just happened." These processes are based on many angles in life for him and I. So, in the beginning I was very curious who lives at 1695 Will Lee Road. Perhaps, it's a couple with children. The address has a similarity to my previous address that got flooded in the year 2020, the 1695 Hwy 177 address, renovated and got sold in March 2022. The Will Lee Road has a similarity to my Cabana, the address is 1680 Will Lee Road. The address 1695 Will Lee Road is the house across my Cabana, 1680 Will Lee Road with many trees and it was difficult to be able to see who lives in my neighborhood. As I am passing by at this address 1695 Will Lee Road, I saw the exact look alike of the van Thomas (my previous husband), and I was supposedly to purchase a white color Van in year 2015 similar to the Van I saw at my neighbor. The van I saw in 1695 Will Lee Road is color beige.

While I was opening my gate coming home from downtown, I

see a man standing by his mailbox taking out mails and I was trying to stare at him to know who my neighbor was. He stared at me but quickly turned his back and walked towards his home. In my mind at that time seeing him at the mailbox "maybe he does not want to know his neighbor" because he just looked at me and left without saying hello.

So, I was also reluctant to greet him to introduce myself as his neighbor. However, there was some kind of energy in me that pushed me in this direction to meet him. Somehow. Despite how many times I passed by his house, I always have this thought of avoidance but one day, my hands maneuvered the wheels of my car to his yard and blew the horn of my car, and I saw him coming from the back of his house. I then introduced myself that I am his neighbor and I now live across from his house.

My reasoning of being reluctant to introduce myself because I am a woman, and in my culture while I was growing up, a man supposedly the first one to introduce himself. I also did not say hello at the mailbox to him because my reasoning in my mind "I am a woman and I considered that a man must say hello to me first before I said hello to a man." I learned that mentality from my parents when I was young. However, in this situation and looking back to all men trying to date me he is very different. The differences between him and other men I met were the way how men approached me.

Other men would aggressively approach a woman for a

different purpose. You know what I meant. This man who lives in 1695 Will Lee Road, my neighbor, approached me in a very different way that it makes me think that he is not like those men I met before. Although introducing myself first, I have never done this before. However, in this situation with my neighbor I somehow comfortable to meet and talk to him because of the way he approached me with confidence, trust, respect, and self-respect.

I introduced myself and I said "Hello, my name is Sofia. I live across the road from your house. He said, "my name is Cameron" with his two arms crossed together approaching me. He was very calm approaching me. He is very tall, 6 feet, blue eyes, and a long nose. I am very small and petite woman and I act like a child, and smiley always. I asked him if he was travelling because he has a huge van. He said yes, and he introduced me to his van. He opened the van door, and I was so surprised because it was complete such as bed, electricity, kitchen, and refrigerator. I asked him a surprising question such as "You did all of these? Wow!" I was amazed at his talent of creating a livable van. We then continued getting to know each other. He travels all over and climbs mountains. I was impressed. Also, he does wood carving making into lamps and bowl made of wood. His van he made all inside the van to be livable. Livable to the point where it was made into a recreational vehicle (RV). I was amazed!

I always watch a man who approaches me based on their

respectful behavior and talents. Cameron approaches me with a respectable manner, in a very calm way. I was very surprised because usually men approach me in very excited behavior, and perhaps I would say aggressive way. The journey begins knowing my neighbor, named Cameron, who climb mountains, and being with Natural Resources and travel all over the USA. He likes to merge with living things in the wild, such as birds, plants, amazement of our Lord's creation such parks, lakes, river, and oceans. Knowing Cameron that day, however, now I know that not all men are like that. Cameron is different than the rest of men I met. The first time I met him I felt respected. Along the days we known each other such as the likes and dislikes, I asked him about how his mountain climbing. He told me he climbed the mountains of Copper Mountain in a Superstition Mountain located in Arizona, and many other mountains. After finding out about him, he invited me to go with him. So, I feel like I am so comfortable with him, so I was very interested in going with him traveling and mountain climbing.

I was excited after hearing him in the phone inviting me to come with him to travel. Two things in my mind that somehow put me on hold. But at the same time I was excited, and jumped to joy after receiving his call to travel with him. However, I must think about it first if I have to go with him traveling. I gathered all what I had observed about him, and I knew I could trust him.

He told me that he will be traveling soon. And he asked me if I would like to come with him. Yes! I said I wanna go! I wanna go! I wanna go! I was so excited. I felt like a child found a friend in my neighborhood. I felt like I was heading in a different direction in my life from being alone and now I have a friend. However, again I would remember my mother who taught me not to engage quickly with a man. Also, *"no sex before marriage"* type of remembrance while growing up as a child to a lady, and now a widow living by myself in my cabana. These words stayed in my mind until the days of my age 60s. I also want to make sure that I can trust him. I calculated all the trustworthy signs from this man. He is a respectful man. We then became friends.

We then moved forward in watching movie in Dothan Alabama AMC theater, and he was next to me in a respectable manner. Not like other men would go forward and take advantage of the time being alone with me. Our friend relationship became closer. He invited me to come with him to travel to North Carolina to visit his sister. However, that day I had to meet the owner of the office I was going to rent in Panama City to reopen my Notary Public office, and art gallery. So, I refused to come with him to North Carolina. However, he is going to continue his travel all the way farther North Carolina. He traveled to Maine and stopped by White Top Mountain in Virginia. He climbed and enjoyed the scenery, then he called me, and I answered his call. He asked me if I wanted to come with him to travel in Main. He told me to fly from Panama City Airport to Pennsylvania. I decided to go because the office that I am going to rent supposedly for my business is not done yet, somehow. He instructed me to what airplane is going to Pennsylvania to meet him there at the airport.

Therefore, I flew from Panama City airport to Pennsylvania for him to pick me up at the airport so we can travel together to Maine and beyond. We camped in Pennsylvania, Adirondack Mountain in New York. We stopped at the lake, and I was swimming in very clear water, I enjoyed it. Meanwhile, Cameron was playing guitar. I remembered a man and his family camping next to us came to appreciate Cameron's guitar play. The man said he could not wait to see Cameron while playing the guitar because he was amazed of the guitar music. Cameron was appreciated by this man.

We then continued to Acadia National Park, and Bar Harbour. We watched the water activities hampering the rocks and it makes a beautiful sound of nature. Our travels continued to many rivers. We swam and jumped to the river, and we kayaked while taking photos of our memories. It was my first kayaking experience. I love it. Thank you, Lord. It didn't end there. We then continued to Maine and went deeper in the woods and stayed for days. We ate fresh lobsters and enjoyed the scenery. I have never been to this kind of activity before.

Such a beautiful experience. We also went fishing, kayaking, paddle boarding, and camping, spending the night where we could see the moon shining brightly on us. We then continued to Michigan, where I met Cameron's relatives, nieces, nephews and sisters and their husbands. Then I trusted him more knowing his sisters meeting them in Michigan. His sisters accepted me as their sisters soon at that moment. We went kayaking in Michigan. What a wonderful experience I had. I cried while I was writing this chapter because I never had sisters when I came to America, and I am far away from my biological sisters. Then I met Cameron's sisters, Jeannie, Alison, and Lynne. As I mentioned previously, I was living by myself alone in my Cabana. I lost my businesses, and I can't find anyone among all the people I knew. I am so thankful for that moment, such a wonderful experience I had with Cameron and his family that will not be forgotten. We kayaked with Cameron's family, and I felt like I was surrounded with loving family members which I had never had since Covid, flooding and death came to my life.

Anyhow, I remembered when we were camping in this river, we had to do barbequing. We had meat in the refrigerator, and I said we don't have a grill. Suddenly, Cameron went to the van and got the package and opened it. I was watching while he was putting this steel thing together no bigger than his shoes. I stared and stared at to comprehend what was that thing he was putting it together. I can't figure it out. Then, my eye squinted to see clearly what he is putting it together. I swayed my shoulder what was he was doing, and I asked what is that he is putting together, and he answered, "It's a grill" a tiny grill only fits in a small meat or two tiny rib eyes pieces. I laughed out loud until my stomach hurt and I needed to drink cold water, that is. I didn't stop laughing. I laughed because the grill was so cute looking, so small. That was a moment I will never forget.

I enjoyed the laughter with him. After traveling with Cameron with so much laughter we encountered, both he proposed to marry me. I was so surprised, but I agreed. Therefore, the marriage was planned. I notified my DoctorSon, but he disagreed because we just met not long ago, and he thought that we just knew each other. I told my son that I came with Cameron camping all over. My son was alarmed and so worried. I then introduced my son to Cameron on the phone, followed by visiting my son in Tallahassee after travels. My son asked so many questions to Cameron.

My Thought Universe carried me to these days of my dream became true. Before meeting Cameron, I was always wished to travel in an RV but I did not fulfill my dreams then due to so many blockage of my life such as responsibilities such as managing my businesses I've opened since in 2004 moving from New Jersey to Panhandle Florida. As an entrepreneur my responsibility is 24 hours 7 days a week type of responsibility. In addition to non-expecting disastrous life experiences such as Covid, flooding, sickness, and death therefore, everything changed in my life that puts my direction to another phase in life. The Lord Almighty's master plan begins.

I now understand God's "Master Plan" I called it. After meeting and knowing Cameron in July 2022, we got married in November2022 and I am enjoying traveling with him. Before we got married, climbs mountains, we go paddle boarding, travel to the Niagra Falls, and to all States to the East, West, North and South. The Lord put me in the direction where I was supposed to belong. Now, my dreams are fulfilled, and I just go along with the flow that easy, and just let it go. I could still remember and understand how a Master Plan of the Lord goes along with us while we are in a chaotic life at that moment, then followed, shall I call it, *"I see the Light, there I came."*

I remember, in the Bible while I am reading every morning and share my prayer to all my members, I can see my life there. I am always thankful. The blessings and abundance in life that the Lord has given me despite those troubles along the way. My husband, Cameron and I always pray every morning and be thankful for all we have. Now, I understand my life. However, it could be that there will be some darkness along the path that we are heading, but always remember that the Lord has always has a Master Plan for every human being. While writing and continuing this book of mine, we are at the Keys in his RV enjoying God's creation on earth. The water flow, the birds, the overall views of the Bahaia Honda State Park. I am thankful to the Lord that I met Cameron, my husband since year 2022. Our traveling activities enjoying God's provisions I truly enjoy it.

My husband, Cameron, is now active in producing art pieces.

He does wood artistry, making lamps, bowls, vases, trays, turn tables, and canvas painting with me. He has a website where you can check his beautiful wood art pieces. His website is www.cameron-adams.com, of his beautiful creations of wood carving. My creation of fine art paintings and my book written and published are all on my website: www.drsofiaadams.com

While enjoying my husband Cameron's company in traveling and camping, I also do my book writing, and painting views we encountered throughout our traveling activities. We will continue these types of activities throughout our living life here on earth of plenty. We then plan to buy property near the ocean, bay, and creek for us to do biking, kayaking, fishing, and blending with the world's beauty. I am thankful to the Lord's Master Plan for us. Amen. As my father used to say, "America Is Heaven" I am here in heaven" enjoying God's provision with my husband Cameron.

Despite the many struggles I went through in my life, I somehow became more productive. You may question why, therefore, let me explain. The struggles we go through in life I would say are maybe the barrier to getting to the other side of life. However, if we can get through the storms in our lives, we can and we will survive. I've been there and I used these struggles experiences as my steppingstone to get to the other side of life. I learned how to jump through rivers, and many ugly terrains and sharp stones.

These wounds and bruises while jumping through fire, became my tools to survival. My explanation may be misunderstood due to using some examples of what's the meaning of the word "struggles." Struggles means hardship in life we all go through. Here on earth, we have roads to travel. However, roads can be very rough to travel, and we quit traveling instead of passing through these roads to get to the other side. I think you understand what I meant.

To this day, I am a published author, and a fine artist, and continuing my volunteering in visiting neglected and abused children in the counties I am assigned to helping communities in life struggles of disunite families which is so common to these days. Cameron, now my husband, is also an artist creating art pieces out of wood taken from our acreage. I am content and enjoying our traveling and activities now in our age at 60s it feels like we are free and comfortable in life facing toward a good life waiting for us both to move forward along the path of humbleness, contained, blessed and abundance. I enjoyed it very much and we are now focusing on AirBnB rental, and we plan to travel internationally also for a purpose of Art and Book Fair Festival events, and we are ready, but only God's willing.

To enforce the understanding of life events and solve the clues in our lives while we journey on this earth of plenty, these similarities happened unintendedly such as when I renovated my cabana, the wall inside and out was silver, gray, the fence was gray color, and the doors were red color. Amazing! Cameron bought a piece of lot in Panacea Silver Glen Phase II. We plan to build a house with property surrounded by water that we can enjoy kayaking, boating, and biking along with the bike trail in this area. Previously, in the month of March was my husband Cameron's 65th birthday and we watched a movie whatever is available at that time we went to the theater in the area, and suddenly the available and showing at that time was movie titled "65" and Cameron was 65 years old and celebrating his 65th birthday watching movie "65." Such an amazing coincidence and synchronicity or shall I say, "is it meant to be?"

Something to think about this, 1695 Hwy 177 and 1695 Will Lee Road as a coincidence in my neighborhood that we somehow get our mail from one another although we didn't know each other before this happened, living in this address since year 2004 and 2006 for Cameron. Somehow, there was a puzzle in this type of coincidence which at that time affected the Post Man of note on top of the mail, "Not Mine" "Wrong Address" or "Return To Sender." These incidents started in the years 2006 to 2020.

Then after Covid, hurricane, sickness, and death of my previous husband, Thomas, I was living by myself. I met Cameron, my neighbor in July 2022. Heading to Panama City for Notary assignment, I saw Cameron at his mailbox, getting his mail but something spiritually connected between me and him, somehow.

Although I didn't say hello to my neighbor, and neither did he say hello to me, the puzzle still lingered in our mind. It could be a puzzle, but it deepened through times passing by his address at 1695 Will Lee Road. We then became friends.

The friendship didn't end there, and we went to dinner and watched movies with always self-respect for each other and set boundaries. I would remember my parents always says, *"No sex before marriage."* Which I have always that in my mind for self-respect and boundaries. However, Cameron proposed to me for us get married. He notifies his relatives, and the preparation was very smooth, and no stress but it was enjoyable. We then created a party before solemnizing the marriage. His sisters, Jeannie, Alison, and Lynn were there and David, our brother-in-law made a video when Cameron was dancing with me. This video included our wedding ceremony on the beach of Fort Walton Beach Florida. You can find our video in YouTube "Cameron and Sofia's Wedding." We got married on the beach barefoot and enjoyed the scenery of the ocean. Such a wonderful experience!

When we got married on November 12, 2022, I wore wedding clothes colored silver gray, and red flowers around our wedding path towards the ocean in Fort Walton Beach where we celebrate and got married promised to each other shall I say, "til death do us part". Also, Cameron's necktie was gray. The red and the silver color represents something for me because it always occurs in my life which when I was young at age 10 years old, I dreamt about silver color airplane and red door which I was a giant trying to hold the airplane flying in the sky. Therefore, at 10 years of age, my father predicted me that I will be going to America and America is heaven. Also, my cabana has red doors and gray walls which I call it such a synchronicity, that is. Yes, it is. Are these coincidences between me and Cameron's experiences? Or maybe it's really the road we both assigned to travel here on earth of the living. We now travel all over enjoying our retirement age. We are blessed. We are thankful to our Lord. Spiritually, shall I say coincidence, or it meant to be?

On April 9, 2023, my husband Cameron had a dream. Early morning after I shared our prayers to all our more than 300 members online, he told me that he had a dream. My husband Cameron dreamed about my previous husband, Thomas, who passed away in December 2020. Cameron's dream was about fishing in the river with my previous husband, Thomas, giving him the fishing rod with the bait with it and to follow him where to fish. While Cameron was looking and checking the fishing rod all the way down at the end next to the bait Cameron found a metal form like a key. Cameron accepted the fishing rod with a form of a key metal attached to it, then Thomas disappeared.

While I was listening to Cameron telling me his dream that day of April 9th at 6:30 in the morning, I was about to cry, but I don't want to ruin the moment of telling me about his dream because in the spiritual world there is a meaning to his dream (Cameron, April 9, 2023). To explain the meaning of this book I will be writing the next story titled: "The Boyman." Boyman story is about the painting I did at Abbeville Lake connecting the Eufaula Lake in Alabama. I bought 2 properties in Abbeville Alabama in year 2004. In the year 2022 Cameron and I went there, and Cameron did paddle boarding in the big lake while I was painting him on canvas. To be continued in my next book titled "The Boyman" because we are the children of God. It is amazing to see and feel God's Master Plan for every human being here on earth of plenty.

These addresses mean a lot to me, 1695 Hwy 177 and 1695 Will Lee Road as a synchronicity in my neighborhood that we somehow get our mail from one another although we didn't know each other then. These incidents or may not be perhaps it meant to be started in the years 2006 to 2020. Then after covid, hurricane, sickness, and death of my previous husband, Thomas when I was living by myself in my cabana a gated 3 acres land, I met Cameron, my neighbor living in 1695 Will Lee Road in July 2022.

I found the love of my life in the world of the living. I got married to Cameron in November 2022. This next life journey of mine is brighter than ever before. My website was created for my books published and art pieces. The beautiful life begins with the man I met at 1695 Will Lee Road.

All I can say is SUCH A BLESSING given by the Almighty! While living here on earth of plenty, a destination we are assigned, the SPIRITUAL connection between soul and spirit in the world of existence. We are now able to see it. I now have sisters here in the USA, Cameron's sisters were accepting me heartfully as their sister. I am thankful. Thank You Sisters, AMAZING GRACE! AMEN!

Editing this manuscript still makes me cry going through life experiences since when I was young and to my now 60s. With Cameron on my side, I can cry on his shoulder, not crying anymore by myself for these special moments of editing my manuscript The Memoir: The River Of Life with someone I can cry on mesmerizing the painful and the beautiful memories in my life. Thank You Lord. The ups and downs in life had given me the skills to survive going through the rough river and terrain of life, and now I am continuing the flow of the water in the river of life with my dear husband Cameron with tears of gratitude.

IN SUMMARY

Life's ups and downs while living here on earth of plenty, there were times we chose our own path. A path against the water flows in the river of life, and we stumble. We let it go and then we got up and let go again. Then we follow what's God's master plan for all humanity. The plan is sufficient to survive through flowing of the water. Through the river of life where there are ups and downs, we then very satisfied, content, and feeling abundance and blessed. We then follow the flow of the river of life.

My mother bore six daughters. I am the third of the six sisters. We only have one set of parents in a lifetime. I am thankful for everything I have and the good experiences and struggles I went through. The experiences I have in life gave me the terrain to follow and knowledge to which to avoid the next step and which one to continue in the next. To me I believe what my father had said when I was young and naïve that "America is heaven" an innocent child of all life activities. However, I made it here in heaven, despite many struggles I had encountered which I called the dark tunnel, I finally came through the light and saw it all.

Through many trials in life, I survived, that's heaven. I continued my education to a higher level and became a published author. I am an artist, and selling some of my books and paintings makes me feel accomplished after all where I am settling myself to life in simplicity. I always think about what I learned in my BA in Art History, *"Less Is More."* I've been through poorness, richness and simplicity acknowledging the abundance and blessings, and now I chose the simplicity of life, the *less is more.*

As the third of among sisters, I was the only one who pursued and fulfilled my dreams to come out from the other side of life. I was determined to improve my life situation, such as traveling to different places to seek opportunities. Despite disastrous and life-cause experiences, somehow, I was able to get through and survive. I found out that through struggles and hardship in life, we become stronger. I used these experiences as stepping stones to move forward. Meaning that through struggles, we learn something to become stronger and more knowledgeable of things. We are strengthened and able to handle the next hardship in life due to our experiences.

Being a Doctor Of Philosophy, I managed and learned the thinking and reasoning of humanity, and the humans' experiences in our journey here on earth of plenty. Such what I been through experiences then I became knowledgeable of the unseen, the thought, good common sense, wisdom, and good consciences, and the strength to survive in this world of chaos, and plenty. Incorporating these life experiences and knowledge I learned to become fruitful in life.

My books are mostly research books, and I have been publishing since 2014. You can purchase these books of mine through www.amazon.com. You can also order my books through my website, www.drsofiaadams.com.   One of my books, titled "Nepotistic Ideology Of Family-Owned Organization," was chosen by Scholar's Press to be published through them. Scholar's Press is an Academic Publishing. Scholar's Press only published those books that are the best selected through examination of the contents. At that time, when they found my manuscript from Capella University, my manuscript was one of ten PhDs to be chosen to be published through Scholar's Press. Again, I found the simplicity of life living here on earth of plenty.

However, it is not too late to enjoy knowing myself, and accredited myself for all I have accomplished in life through hard work, and persistence. Now in my 60s years of age, I am enjoying myself with my new companion, Cameron whom I met in July 2022 and got married in November 2022. Cameron is a man with joy within him. He loves to encounter the beauty of natural resources. He enjoys traveling, tapping into knowing the resources we have here on earth of plenty as blessings we have received. Enjoying the scenery throughout by traveling is such beautiful living. The next book I am going to put together will be titled "The Boyman." It is about a man who brings out his boynism from within him that makes his surrounding enjoyable and pleasant.

DR. SOFIA LAURDEN-DAVIS ADAMS' BIOGRAPHY

Sofia Laurden-Davis Adams is a PhDs in Human Services specialized in Management in Nonprofit Agencies and Leadership graduated in April 2014 at Capella University. Dr. Adams is currently an Independent Contractor with mortgage, bank, law, and title companies function as a Certified Signing Specialist. She has 2 sons, Rhoss (Junjun) 41, and Danny (Jr) 34 years of age. Both sons are married, and currently she has six grandchildren. Rhoss works in logistics, and Danny is a medical doctor.

Since 1989, Dr. Sofia Laurden-Davis Adams worked in the banking and real estate industries. At the beginning of the year 2000, she became an Independent Contractor working part-time while pursuing her education. Currently, she is an entrepreneur and a volunteer of Guardian Ad Litem, serving as the voice for neglected and abused children in three counties in Panhandle, Florida. She taught 4th & 5th religious education in the church she attended. She teaches art classes and offers "Courtesy Art Classes," and she travels to art students' selected locations, and classes can be held in her own Fine Art Studio. She is an Independent Contractor performing signings for mortgage, bank, and title companies.

Dr. Adams graduated as a Doctor of Philosophy (PhDs) in April 2014. In 2006 she graduated with a master's degree in human resource management from the University of Phoenix. She has a bachelor's degree major in Art History, and Studio Art at Georgian Court University in New Jersey graduated in 2004, and an associate degree in liberal arts doubled with Photography at Brookdale Community College graduated in 2000. She moved from Bricktown, New Jersey to Bonifay Florida in 2004.

The same year, she developed a 501 C3 organization named Bonifay Guild for the Arts, Inc. which in year 2010 this organization was renamed to Laurden-Davis & Associates sole proprietorship consists of Mobile Signing Agent, Notary Public, Fine Art Studio, Online Art Gallery, and Rental Properties. Dr. Adams developed a yearbook for her previous organization titled, "Memorable Moments of Bonifay

Guild for the Arts, Inc. Part 1" The book has 110 pages of compiled photos, stories, and activities of Bonifay Guild for the Arts, Inc. The yearbook copies were placed at Chambers of Commerce, and libraries for previous BGA and LDA members' keepsakes.

Dr. Sofia Laurden-Davis Adams and her husband Cameron plan to travel internationally. She plans to continue writing books and curricula and, as an independent contractor, function as an art teacher and certified Signing Specialist. Dr. Adams published her books since the year 2014 to this day. Check her next books at www.amazon.com also on her website: www.drsofiaadams.com. Cameron makes artwork out of pieces of wood, such as lamps, bowls, etc. See his website at www.Cameron-adams.com

DR. SOFIA's POETRY OF THE RIVER OF LIFE

MY PAPA AND THE BLACK BIRD

My papa was a photographer. I believed that he could make the big black bird unable to fly. This black bird was sitting on the avocado tree on the side of our ancient house. The front of the house faced the main road. The left side of the house, a well-built-in decade ago before we moved into this ancient house. We pitched water from this well for cooking and drinking.

On the right side of the house, a big avocado tree grew from five decades ago, before we moved into this ancient house. This avocado tree with lively, green, shiny leaves and fruits, there, the big black bird lived. Under the avocado tree, there was the black bird's waste and seeds of what it eats. My Lola, meaning grandma word in the Philippines, used to say, if you try to stay there and get some avocado fruit or stands under this big tree, you would be cursed. Like, you will become a black bird just like the black bird living up in this tree.

One day, I was crying because my sister was picking on me calling me a "cry baby." My father rescued me from all these "sisters teasing" things and promised to tell me a story-a real story. I sat on his lap and told me a story about his "oracion." Oracion is a Spanish word. Meaning, "magic" or "power" I was very eager to listen to my papa's story about using "oracion" to the big black bird perched on avocado tree.

"Papa, tell me a story now. What are you waiting for?" I asked. My paper just looked at the big avocado tree and stared at it. "Papa, tell me a story now," I spoke. He lifted his right hand, put his forefinger on his mouth and said, "Shhhh. Quiet, I am waiting for the blackbird to perch on the avocado tree. Here it comes, come one, birdy, come on." It was six o'clock at night. After supper, the whole family would sit outside on the porch to watch the blackbird living in the avocado tree. This time, my papa and I were outside on the porch watching this big creature.

My papa stared and stared at the avocado tree. Putting his both forefingers on his forehead, and he said the words I could not understand. Suddenly, the black bird fell on the ground, and tried to recover by waving its wings, but just laid down on the ground and stopped breathing, I thought. It was dark, there were no lights on the street, all I could see was the big creature lying down on the ground. I tried to squeeze my eyes with my both fingers to make sure I was not dreaming. I saw the big black bird on the ground lying. I was speechless. I was stunned. I could not move; I was stuck, and I was amazed. How did my papa do that! The next morning, I went outside to look at the big bird for the first time in the bright sunlight. "Papa! Papa! come on papa, come down here." I spoke. All my sisters came down to see the bird lying on the ground. Thinking how papa made the big bird unable to fly by just using his two fingers on both sides of his forehead. My papa was coming too, to see the black bird for the first time under the sunlight that he thought he made it believing he had a power.

"Papa, the black bird is not here. Where is it papa, where is it." I asked, confused. My papa just looked at me and smiled with a question in his mind and said nothing. My sisters were laughing and went back inside the house. It seemed as if they never care where the big black bird was living or if it was still alive. I was left alone and worried where the big black bird was headed. It's been a long time now. It's been forty-seven years. It is still vivid in my mind. I still did not understand where the big black bird could have gone. I was living in Hawaii in 1991 when my father died. I went home after I received the telegram that my Papa passed away. I went back to Philippines quickly.

"Moan and groan" of my father's death, I did not forget to ask him the question I had since when I was eight. In his coffin, I asked. "Papa where did the big black bird go.? I cried. At forty-one years of age, would I still believe that my papa really had the power to make the bird unable to fly? We have so many questions in our mind that never were answered? We as human beings tend to separate our minds and spirits from the ones we love and respect. There are so many questions we may not have answers to. Then, we realized, it's too late to ask. Maybe, the beauty of it is a mystery.

(END)

<u>ENJOYING THE OCEAN</u>

As the wind blows in the never-ending ocean. People running around and applying some lotion. Wearing bikinis and swimming trunks. And suddenly here comes a fearless skunk. A fisherman with a long fishing rod. Trying to catch some slippery cod. People at the beach are having fun. Using an umbrella under the sun.

But where is the skunk? He is out in the ocean, also wearing his swimming trunk. When the fisherman was done fishing, awe all the people started to get itching. Maybe it was their clothes. Maybe nobody knows that they were just bitching.

<u>(END)</u>

Dr. Sofia Laurden-Davis Adams

THE SONG I PLAYED

When I was alone in the dark room, I went to my piano and played the song. Sunrise, Sunset was the title I played. I noticed my tears reappeared. The song was meaningful to hear. The following set of music on the keyboard. I Lost my timing, voice, and eyes full of tears. Take time to play and give love to your children because tomorrow will never be the same. The lyrics tell me, "When did he grow to be so tall? Wasn't it yesterday when he was so small"?

Move on, fly your wings, and be happy. Wake up in the morning, creating another yesterday. Rise, and fall, these are the experiences you will have. Don't forget the yesterdays you have left. Helping hands are ready to hold your nest. Go fly high with your wings already been created. Most had been formed and suited. Fly high and reach the sky to follow your dream. That you've been dreaming since then. Goodbye, goodbye I will see you when you are up in the sky.

<u>(END)</u>

SCARS

Is this you? Maybe the images of your past? Who is he? And who is the person looking down to the water to mirror? If you touch the water mirror, it wiggles. It became blurry and you can't tell who it is anymore. You've guessed. Hmmm! You think it is not you but only the images of your past. Now, you've realized that it was yesterday's creation you've left behind.

But you were trying to pretend, it didn't happen. You sit near the river where the water you've mirrored. After you have touched it, you were waiting to clear the water that wiggles. It took a while before it cleared. Suddenly came the two images in the water mirror. As you look at it, you see yourself and your son together. And now, you've remembered what had happened.

You rebelled and took action. You didn't realize you are only hurting your creation. You think you are hurting someone for revenge. But clearly, you are hurting yourself, and your son, again, and again. After all, the images of the water mirror would become blurry again.

Also, it might be too late to clear the disturbed water all over. Didn't you see? You are just going around the circle! Circle has no ending, hoping you would remember, Remembered, and realized that those images would become blurry If you would touch it and hoped to remember even the pain that colored purple, that is insane!

(END)

Dr. Sofia Laurden-Davis Adams

THE FLICKERING TREES

As we traveled on Highway 539. We had fun and a very good time. The flickering rays showered through the trees. Opened the window and felt a cool breeze. And I see the flickering trees. We noticed the sun glistening through the haze as we made our way on the road and gazed.

Down long, long road of travel I have found. Life is a struggle, it may sound. And I can see the flickering trees. Abandoned broken, rusty boat found along the roadside. People must have left it and move on and go on with their lives. The flickering sun rays through tall, short trees.

It tells me, we are on our way to a brighter day. And I see the flickering trees. Life has ups and downs, like a light flickering, dark and bright. My eyes must be blind when the flickering light shines. I couldn't see when it hit the trees. Life could be the same, as the flickering ray's movement explains. Again, I see the flickering trees. There is this space that has no trees. The sunshine was so bright without a trace. A long journey of life can be a flickering light.

Suddenly, I see the flickering trees. Driving along the ups and downs, winding road. The sun, and the rays following us with the mode. Dancing, fencing, jiggling, laughing. Sunrays, come along, we want to be followed. And I see the flickering trees.

<u>(END)</u>

<u>THE PARADIGM</u>

See, if we are living by ourselves alone. We tend to believe in our own belief whether right or wrong. No one will disagree and agree. We don't know the difference, the cause, and the effect of it.

There will be no arguments and no decision-making. There will be no hold-back and no forward-looking. Only the time when we are with someone, something funny, something odd, something missing, do we feel it, but feel ignorant of all the things. Now, it's time to change, but it will take time to renew and blossom because it was too late to socialize and to admit the decision we had made before things happened.

Going back to your room "thinking," Why! Am I back again? Maybe because it was our pattern that when we get hurt, it is easier to live alone.

Lying on your bed, analyzing and organizing things in your head. Your feet are on top of two pillows, one pillow underneath your head, two palms on top of the pillow, and your head, skull, and brain under your palm, protecting from thinking so hard about what to do. Now, you're going out of your room, mingling with others to test yourself again. To see if you know what they are talking about. There are so many things to explore and learn; the time is too short to cover the whole paradigm. It seems we learn from others and hear their ideas and decision-making. Even though it's too late for us to learn other things, it is not too late to listen to them. Your smile came, and the day brightened because now you understand the paradigm that you've been missing.

(END)

Dr. Sofia Laurden-Davis Adams

<u>SHADES</u>

Are you satisfied with what you have done? Did you look thoroughly to see what was behind the screen? You see blood of your blood, but the shade covers everything, unable you to recognize what you have done to yourself and to your son. You remember the past when you were young. You thought this might be the right thing to do, just like what your father had done to you. Again, the shade covers everything. I said to you, "You have to go to your father's invitation." You said a big "No." "I hate him so much," you said. You continued, "I don't even want to talk to him. He left my mom when I was little, and they even gave her to my grandmother. So, my grandmother must take care of me." I said, "Maybe he has changed now. You must try to talk to him." You responded with confusion, "I don't know how I could talk to him. I don't feel like talking to him at all." And I said to you, "Your feeling of hate for your father continues." Is that what you wanted?

<u>(END)</u>

Dr. Sofia Laurden-Davis Adams

THE BOYMAN

Kayaking, boarding, paddling and enjoying the water at Abbeville Lake. The Boyman heading to the deep ocean with just like a piece of cake. For me it's scary, but the Boyman keeps going with peace and joy must be.

Loving the water and pushing through the deep side seems so easy. I want to come and join you to have some fun, although the day was too hazy. Through the painting, I have painted for this man. Seeing the painting on the canvas, someone commented it was such a joyful boy paddling.

Enjoying the water, he then called this man a Boyman as it may seem. The joy, laughter, and heart and mind of Boymanism towards a life of a good living. I was then very much amazed by the Boyman's pleasant activities. Here I am joining this Boyman who I married just last month.

After learning from the Boyman, traveling, enjoying paddling boarding at Abbeville Lake for the Boyman this one too is just a piece of cake. Life is so beautiful carrying a kayak with the Boyman who I appreciate. Across the water he skated, and I could not tell his age whether a sixty-eight or eight!

I had such a good feeling of my age now in 60s, I am then excited to join Boyman's activities. Paddling, Kayaking, and swimming in the deep oceans and river, I see mantes like the Boyman so happy there is.

(END)

Dr. Sofia Laurden-Davis Adams

THE MICRO-LEVEL SCREAM

The United States of America, the wealthiest nation in the world, hear your people out crying. Save the people from drowning on the poverty line. It is like in the water, people are slowly going down--down--to the deeper side of the poverty sign.   Workers worked so hard but remained in the position just to afford life necessities to live long. Poor people would like to run away from it, but the quicksand ate them all up. The quicksand spits them all, seems to let them go, and come back once poor people have something, so they'll be eaten up again.

The whole body was exhausted and suffer from fatigue, working so hard no time to rest--work--just to get by and get some "For Sale" bread. People work so hard just to pay bills and groceries for food, just to get by and to live. Look at the single parents, and the children, the elderly, and the homeless, and the jobless. The people pick up someone else's trash to sell, to get some money to buy and to live.

People who work at the Flea Markets pray and hope people will stop by their table to buy something because their children are waiting at home, expecting the single mother would come home with groceries of food. Looking for a "For Sale" sign, make sure the coins spent will last long. Found a loaf of bread that expired two months ago. She would rather take it because it is cheap, and from coins, the single mother has some change left.

What are the reasons for all this? "They ensure that society's dirty work gets done; the poor subsidize the middle and upper classes by working for low wages; the poor buy goods and services that would otherwise be rejected (such as day-old bread, used car, and the services of the old, retired, or incompetent "professional" and the poor, being politically powerless, can be forced to absorb the costs of change and growth in the American society" on this earth of plenty we may say. (Benokraitis 388).

(END)

THE HARVEST OF THE EARTH

I looked, and there before me was a white cloud, and seated on the cloud was one "like a son of man" With a crown of gold on his head and a sharp sickle in his hand. Then, another angel came out of the temple. And called in a loud voice to him who was sitting on the cloud, "Take your sickle and reap because the time to reap has come, For the harvest of the earth is ripe." So, he, who was seated on the cloud, swung his sickle over the earth, and the earth was harvested. (Revelation 16:14,15).

(END)

THE POWER OF NATURE

After I exercise, I listen to nature songs. I saw water flowing in the river, crystal rain drops on the leaves, birds and crickets chirping, frogs singing beautiful songs that nobody understands, just the sound of it. When you hear all these soothing sounds of nature, you will feel relaxed and at ease.

One day, when it was my lunchtime, I went to the creek here in Fort Monmouth, near where my husband works, just to watch birds flying and water running in the stream. When the wind blew, trees were touching each branch to reach out to each other. I said to myself, "Maybe that's the way they communicate with each other." While I was there, sitting on the bench with a table, chin on my palms, my elbows leaning on the table, thinking, and I said, "Birds have no problems." I was watching birds flying up in the sky, up all the way down and touching the water in the stream. I said to myself, "Maybe that's how they take showers." I smiled and laughed to myself. It seems like they are showing me that life has ups and downs.

One bird was playing in the water. The bird's beck and its feathered body went all the way to the cold water in the stream. I think they were telling me to "cool it down, Sofia." It seems like I was talking to them. I felt the cold blow of the wind telling me to get up and get my coat in the car. Nature doesn't want me to get sick, I guess. While I was walking towards my car, I saw an old man come and feed the birds. I was watching them while they were eating. They were very happy that somebody gave food for them to eat. It was getting windy, telling me it was time to go back to work.

One hour of time meant a lot to me that day. I felt like I was in another world. I felt relaxed at that moment; my worries were all gone. The power of nature is very important to people, especially people who work every day, people on the go, those who work in the city, and people who have problems. It is therapy for me. I always have my nature song playing every time I finish exercising. That's the Power Of Nature.

(END)

Dr. Sofia Laurden-Davis Adams

THE REGROWTH

One day, I felt like everything was falling on me. I wept and grieved about my life seems I am not free. Feeling alone and devastated by the flow of the river of life through me and with me being by myself in every problem comes to me it's like I am going down, down to the ground.

On the road of my life, I felt alone, with no one there with me solving issues of every chaos. I examined myself and studied who I am today. After all, disastrous life came to hassle me and gave me struggles that I couldn't contain. I was a happier person than before until recently I went through many disastrous experiences.

However, I've lost all my businesses due to COVID-19, flooding, sickness, and death. After all these experiences, which took a while to recover, the feeling of newness came, thinking about what was going on. I then let it go and let it be the regrowth of my life and situation. It's just happened. I may not have understood it in the beginning, but now I can see the seeds growing healthier and further moving along while the river of life just flows without any hesitation.

(END)

I KNOW THE MEANING OF TRUE LOVE

Love, it sounds like there is no problem in the world if all people know what love is. "Love One Another," what does it mean? I'm confused. Right now, I cannot express love if I base it on what I have experienced. I just can't figure out why it is so complicated. I was numb about this thing.

My two children are the most important people in my life now. I realized they needed my true love and attention. I neglected them for a while due to busyness in life, earning income to afford necessities. I opened my eyes and realized that there were two human beings that needed my true love. I'll make sure they pass on the right path in life.

I will take care of them until they can stand up on their own feet. Even if they've grown up, I will still be available to guide them.

Yes, I do know what love is. Love is you make sure the person that you love is safe from harm. You will be very patient. You don't get jealous. You trust him/her in every way. You will be faithful. Yes, I do know what love is now.

(END)

Dr. Sofia Laurden-Davis Adams

To The Man and The Boys

For when I had a long travel…Now it's time for me stay in one place, place maybe this river, the river where I can tell you… What I have been through, and the struggles I've encountered. In this river, I am the master. The raging water, the flood, and the storm—my boys—. These are only a few for you to learn. Life, just like water, sometimes blurry, sometimes clear. Someone passes along. Paddle the water for them to move on. "Where does the water go?" The boys asked. I responded, "it goes a long way— a long, long way---. To connect the ocean and goes to the big sea. The water has no ending. Unless the soil and land divides… Until it ends—and stops—and can't go anywhere.

Until the breeze ends and can't smell anymore fresh flowers. If the breeze becomes wind…Wind becomes storms to others. Maybe, the next life, just a start, and the beginning of the new life together. In the stream…the water goes in one direction. But it will overflow once there is a storm. My boys—just remember –how to learn and master the river. Once you know how to master the river, water becomes clearer, and life's journey will be smoother, beautiful and to manage is much easier. Remember, you have a long way to go. This river will end. But you my boys will still go on…Until the end of the ocean, and if the soil-- divides the land.

(END)